Good & Evil and the Human Condition

THE CATHOLIC FAITH SERIES

Volume Four

Libreria Editrice Vaticana

United States Conference of Catholic Bishops
Washington, DC

ISBN 978-1-60137-340-3

First printing, December 2012

Contents

Preface

How did the project for this book come about?

For about three years, I have been placing in the Basilica of San Carlo al Corso (Rome), of which I am rector, some catechetical pamphlets on topics related to current events, available to anyone who comes into the basilica. And to my surprise I noticed that more than 2.5 million pamphlets have been taken by people passing through the basilica. So in response to the demand from so many people, I decided to collect, in a compact and portable format, the pamphlets in question.

What criterion was used to select the topics?

The criterion of relevance. I decided to present brief summaries of what the Catholic Church teaches about some of the timely topics that are being brought to people's attention now for various reasons. In some cases I have also tried to select topics that are somewhat forgotten by many Christians today, or even disputed by some of them.

What documents were used in addressing these topics?

Mainly the documents of the Holy See, and for two reasons. First, because these documents tend to be overlooked by the general public, and their richness, comprehensiveness, and beauty deserve to be more widely known. Second, because they express essential and fundamental beliefs that are held not by any one Catholic alone, but by the Catholic Church as a whole, transmitted through the Magisterium of the pope and the bishops. This Magisterium was established by Christ himself, to confirm the faith of individual believers in him so that down through the centuries and in various parts of the world all may profess one and the same Catholic faith.

Why are the topics presented in dialogue form?

From an editorial point of view, the topics are presented in the form of a dialogue, with questions followed by briefly summarized answers.

This dialogue form tends to be more inviting for the reader, and also continues a constant and long-standing catechetical tradition in the history of the Church. Many catechisms that have formed entire generations have used, and very fruitfully, this didactical system of question and answer.

It must also not be forgotten that the Christian faith itself, a special gift from God, is a continual dialogue of God with man, and of man with God.

I also think that it corresponds to the needs of the contemporary world, in which journalistic-style interviews are preferred, as well as summarized formulations, partly because of the little time that many people, even those who identify themselves as Catholic, now set aside for the catechetical study of their own faith. And this lack of time unfortunately leads to religious ignorance, which in turn leads to widespread relativism, to an arbitrary subjectivism, and last but not least to a distressing vacuum of knowledge about the contents of the faith, which characterizes not only children and young people in their catechetical journey but also adults in their varied and demanding activities.

What is the purpose of this book?

It may help people to understand better the beauty and the importance of the response that the Christian faith offers to all on some topics that characterize our society even today.

This book contains only some of the elements that make up the rich and mysterious panorama of the Catholic faith, and only some of the problems that are eating away at the world today. At the same time, I want to emphasize that in dealing with the individual topics, I do not intend to present all of their aspects and elements, and therefore I do not mean to give each argument exhaustive and complete treatment, but to offer only a few thoughts, fragments of reflection.

So it is intended both for Christians, whom it may provide with an opportunity for a better and deeper understanding of the elements of their faith, and for anyone who might wish to know what the Catholic Church, through some of its official documents, believes and lives, with the help of God.

His Excellency Raffaello Martinelli
Bishop of Frascati
Frascati, September 12, 2010
First anniversary of my episcopal ordination

I
How to Become Saints

What does it mean to be a saint?

It means to be united, in Christ, with God, perfect and holy.

"So be perfect, just as your heavenly Father is perfect" (Mt 5:48), is our command from Jesus Christ, Son of God. "This is the will of God, your holiness" (1 Thes 4:3).

Why does God want us to be holy?

Because God has created us "in our image, after our likeness" (Gn 1:26), and therefore says, "You shall make and keep yourselves holy, because I am holy" (Lv 11:44). "As he who called you is holy, be holy yourselves in every aspect of your conduct" (1 Pt 1:15).

The holiness of God is the origin, the source, the model of all holiness. And moreover, in Baptism, he makes us share in the divine nature, adopting us as his children. And thus he wants his children to be holy as he is holy.

Are we all called to Christian holiness?

"Holiness is not a luxury, it is not a privilege for the few, an impossible goal for an ordinary person; it is actually the common destiny of all men called to be children of God, the universal vocation of all the baptized. Holiness is offered to all." (Pope Benedict XVI, General audience, August 20, 2008). Every Christian is called to holiness, which is "the fullness of Christian life and the perfection of charity and it is brought about by intimate union with Christ and, in him, with the most Holy Trinity. The path to holiness for a Christian goes by way of the cross and will come to its fulfillment in the final resurrection of the just, in which God will be all in all" (*Compendium of the Catechism of the Catholic Church* [*Compendium of the* CCC], no. 428).

How is holiness possible?

✠ The Christian is already holy, by virtue of Baptism. Holiness is inseparably connected to the baptismal vocation of every Christian. In the waters of Baptism, in fact, we have been "washed . . . sanctified . . . justified in the name of the Lord Jesus Christ and in the Spirit of our God" (1 Cor 6:11). We have really been made children of God and partakers in the divine nature, and therefore truly holy.

✠ And precisely because we are holy sacramentally (ontologically, on the level of our Christian being), it is necessary that we also become holy morally—in our thinking, speaking, and acting throughout every day, every moment of our lives. The apostle Paul admonishes us to live "as is fitting among holy ones" (Eph 5:3), to "put on then, as God's chosen ones, holy and beloved, heartfelt compassion, kindness, humility, gentleness, and patience" (Col 3:12).

We must, with God's help, maintain, manifest, and perfect in our lives the holiness that we have received in Baptism: *Become what you are*, this is everyone's task.

✠ This task can be realized by imitating Jesus Christ: the way, the truth, and the life; model, author, and perfecter of all holiness. He is the way of holiness. We are therefore urged to follow his example and conform to his image, obedient in everything as he was to the will of the Father; to have the same sentiments that were in Christ Jesus, who "emptied himself, taking the form of a slave . . . becoming obedient to death" (Phil 2:7-8), and for our sake "became poor although he was rich" (2 Cor 8:9).

✠ Imitating Christ and becoming holy is made possible by the presence in us of the Holy Spirit, who is the soul of the manifold holiness of the Church and of every Christian. It is the Holy Spirit, in fact, who moves us from within to love God with all our heart, with all our soul, with all our mind, and with all our strength (see Mk 12:30), and to love one another as Christ has loved us (see Jn 13:34).

What are the means of our sanctification?

The first and most necessary means is love, which God has poured out in our hearts through the Holy Spirit who has been given to us (see Rom 5:5), and through whom we love God above all things and our neighbor out of love for him. But in order that love "as good seed, is to grow and bring forth fruit in the soul, each one of the faithful must willingly hear the Word of God and with the help of His grace act to fulfill His Will. Each must share frequently in the sacraments, the Eucharist especially, and in liturgical rites. Each must apply himself constantly to prayer, self-denial, active brotherly service, and the exercise of all the virtues. For charity, as the bond of perfection and the fulfillment of the law (cf. Col 3:14; Rom 13:10) rules over all the means of attaining holiness, gives life to them, and makes them work. Hence it is the love of God and of neighbor which points out the true disciple of Christ" (*Lumen Gentium*, no. 42).

Every believer is helped along the journey of holiness by sacramental grace, given by Christ and specific to each sacrament.

Are there various modes and forms of holiness?

Of course. Everyone can and must become holy according to his or her own gifts and responsibilities, in the conditions, duties, and circumstances of his or her own life.

So there are various paths of holiness, suited to each person's vocation. Many Christians, and many laypeople among them, are sanctified in the most ordinary conditions of life.

Why is the Church holy?

✠ The Church is holy because

- God Most Holy is its founder
- In it is present Christ, the head of the Church, who has given himself for it, to sanctify it and make it a source of sanctity
- It is animated by the Holy Spirit, who enlivens it with charity and enriches it with its charisms
- In it the Word of God is preserved faithfully
- In it is found the fullness of the means of salvation. It is the instrument of sanctification through the proclamation of the Word of God, the celebration of the sacraments, the exercise of charity in the constant search for the face of Christ in every brother or sister. The Church is the home of the holiness and charity of Christ poured out by the Holy Spirit, and constitutes its soul.
- The holiness of the Church is the source of the sanctification of its children. Therefore the Church is rightly called the mother of the saints, the one who gives birth to holiness with fertile and magnanimous superabundance.
- It numbers among its ranks the Virgin Mary: in her, the Church is already all-holy. In the Blessed Virgin, the Church has already attained the holiness that makes it without stain and without wrinkle.
- In the Church, throughout all the centuries of its history, Christian holiness has blossomed in an

incredibly extraordinary manner, both heroic and ordinary holiness, producing countless saints
- It has generated, throughout its entire history, endless works of charity

✠ "The holiness of the Church is also fostered in a special way by the observance of the manifold counsels proposed in the gospel by Our Lord to His disciples. Outstanding among them is that precious gift of divine grace which the Father gives to some men (cf. Mt 19:11; 1 Cor 7:7) so that by virginity, or celibacy, they can more easily devote their entire selves to God alone with undivided heart (cf. 1 Cor 7:32-34). This total continence embraced on behalf of the kingdom of heaven has always been held in particular honor by the Church as being a sign of charity and stimulus towards it, as well as a unique fountain of spiritual fertility in the world." (*Lumen Gentium*, no. 42).

✠ The holiness of the Church is

- Essential for the Church
- The fullness of Christian life, lived in relationship with God
- The goal toward which everything else is directed
- The true glory of God
- The most effective proof of the Church's credibility

✠ The Church is indeed holy, but at the same time it is always in need of purification. In fact, all of its members here on earth recognize that they are sinners, always in need of conversion and purification. The Church clasps to its bosom fragile persons who recognize that they are sinners and therefore in need of asking for and receiving God's forgiveness for their sins.

Therefore the Church suffers and does penance for these sins, which it has the power to heal in its children with the Blood of Christ and the gift of the Spirit.

Why does the Church proclaim some of its children saints?

"By canonizing some of the faithful, i.e., by solemnly proclaiming that they practiced heroic virtue and lived in fidelity to God's grace, the Church recognizes the power of the Spirit of holiness within her and sustains the hope of believers by proposing the saints to them as models and intercessors" (*Catechism of the Catholic Church* [CCC], no. 828).

From the beginning, the Church has always believed that the apostles and martyrs are closely united with us in Christ, has celebrated them with particular veneration together with the Blessed Virgin Mary and the angels, and has devoutly implored their intercession. And throughout the centuries, it has always presented for the imitation of the faithful, for veneration and invocation, certain men and women who are shining examples of charity and of all the other evangelical virtues.

What objections are made against the saints?

Some insinuate that they are part of an expansionist strategy on the part of the Catholic Church. For others, the presentation of new saints and blesseds, so diversified by category, nationality, and culture, is nothing but a marketing operation of holiness with the intention of promoting the leadership of the papacy in present-day civil society. There are, finally, some who see canonizations and devotion to the saints as an anachronistic remnant of religious triumphalism, foreign or even contrary to the spirit and letter of Vatican Council II, which put so much emphasis on the vocation of all Christians to holiness.

Those who make these objections do not take into proper account the great role and the true importance of the saints in the Church.

Who are the saints, for the Church?

✠ The saints are

- Those who already contemplate clearly the One and Triune God. Citizens of the heavenly Jerusalem, they ceaselessly sing of the glory and mercy of God, having already made their Paschal passage from this world to the Father.
- "As the colors of the spectrum in relation to the light" (the description of French writer Jean Guitton), because the tonality and accents proper to each one reflect the light of the holiness of God
- Illustrious disciples of the Lord. Origen affirms this decisively: "The saints are an image of the image, the Son being the image" (*On Prayer*, 22, 4). They are a reflection of the light of the Risen Christ. Like the face of a child in which one of the parent's features can

be clearly seen, in that of the saint the contours of the face of Christ have found a new modality of expression.

- Models of evangelical life whose heroic virtues the Church has recognized, recommending that we imitate them. They are an embodiment of the Gospel in everyday life and therefore truly represent a way for us to come into contact with Christ. They "have always been the source and origin of renewal in the most difficult circumstances in the Church's history." (Pope John Paul II, *Christifideles Laici*, no. 16). "They save the Church from mediocrity, they reform it from within, they urge it to be what it must be, the bride of Christ without stain or wrinkle (cf. Eph 5:27)" (Pope John Paul II, Speech to the young people of Lucca, September 23, 1989). And Cardinal Joseph Ratzinger rightly affirmed that "it is not the sporadic majorities which form in the Church here and there that determine the path she and we will take. The saints are the true, crucial majority, and it is from them that we take our bearings. Let us stick to them! They express the divine in the human, the eternal in time."
- Historical witnesses to the universal call to holiness. Preeminent fruit of the redemption of Christ, they are proof that God, at all times and among all peoples, in the most varied sociocultural conditions and in the various states of life, calls his children to attain the perfect stature of Christ (see Eph 4:13; Col 1:28). They demonstrate that holiness is accessible to the multitudes, indeed to every person, and that holiness

can therefore be imitated. With their personal and historical concreteness, they show that the Gospel and new life in Christ are not a utopia or a mere system of values, but are "leaven" and "salt" capable of bringing the Christian faith to life within and from within the different cultures, geographical areas, and historical periods.

- An expression of the catholicity or universality of the Christian faith and of the Church that lives out, guards, and spreads that faith. "The wind blows where it wills, and you can hear the sound it makes, but you do not know where it comes from or where it goes; so it is with everyone who is born of the Spirit" (Jn 3:8). The saints are an expression of that same Spirit and have lived the same faith. This internationalism confirms that holiness does not have boundaries and that it is not dead in the Church; on the contrary, it remains vibrantly relevant. The world changes, but the saints, although they themselves change with the changing world, always represent the same living face of Christ. They shine upon the world a reflection of the light of God, they are visible witnesses of the mysterious and universal holiness of the Church.
- An authentic and constant form of evangelization and of Magisterium. The Church wants to combine the preaching of the truths and values of the Gospel with the presentation of the saints who have lived out those truths and values in an exemplary way.

- People who give glory to God while honoring the human person, because "the glory of God is the human person fully alive" (St. Irenaeus)
- A sign of the capacity of the Christian faith and the Church to be inculturated in the lives of various peoples and cultures
- Intercessors and friends of the faithful who are still pilgrims on the earth, because the saints, although they are immersed in the beatitude of God, know the yearnings of their brothers and sisters and accompany their journey with prayer and support
- Cultural innovators. The saints have made possible the creation of new cultural models, new answers to the problems and the great challenges of the peoples, new developments of humanity in the journey of history. The saints are like beacons: they have shown others the possibilities inherent in human nature. This makes them interesting in terms of culture as well. A great French philosopher of the twentieth century, Henri Bergson, observed that "the greatest figures of history are not the conquerors, but the saints."

✠ The Church confesses all of this when it proclaims, in gratitude to God the Father, "By their [the saints'] way of life you offer us an example, by communion with them you give us companionship, by their intercession, sure support" (Preface I of Saints, *The Roman Missal*).

✠ "Visiting a botanical nursery garden, one is amazed by the variety of plants and flowers, and often one is drawn to think of the imagination of the Creator who has given the earth a wonderful garden. A similar feeling of wonder strikes us when we consider the spectacle of sainthood: the world appears to us as a 'garden,' where the Spirit of God has given life with admirable imagination to a multitude of men and women Saints, of every age and social condition, of every language, people and culture. Every one is different from the other, each unique in his/her own personality and spiritual charism. All of them, however, were impressed with the 'seal' of Jesus (cf. Rev 7:3) or the imprint of his love witnessed through the Cross. They are all in joy, in a festival without end, but, like Jesus, they achieved this goal passing through difficulties and trials (cf. Rev 7:14), each of them shouldering their own share of sacrifice in order to participate in the glory of the Resurrection" (Pope Benedict XVI, *Angelus*, November 1, 2008).

What is the difference between a saint and a blessed?

✠ As for the certainty that both the one and the other is in heaven, there is no difference between them at all.

✠ As for the procedure: Normally a Christian is proclaimed blessed first (beatification), and then, possibly afterward, is proclaimed a saint (canonization).

✠ As for the authority employed in declaring someone a blessed or a saint, it is always the pope who, with a specific pontifical act, declares a blessed or a saint.

✠ As for devotion to them:

- Devotion to a blessed is permitted rather than prescribed, and is limited to a particular diocese or congregation. Without permission from the Holy See, blesseds cannot be named patrons, nor can churches or chapels be named after them, nor can altars be consecrated to them, nor can their feast days be included in the national or diocesan calendar. They can be depicted with the halo, but not with the [crown] proper to the saints.
- Canonization extends devotion to the whole Church, prescriptively, with a definitive proclamation. The canonized can have churches and altars dedicated to them, can be chosen as patrons, and their relics can be venerated in all of the churches.

Are there too many saints and blesseds?

✠ John Paul II responded to this objection as follows: "It is sometimes said that there are too many beatifications today. However, in addition to reflecting reality, which by God's grace is what it is, it also responds to the desire expressed by the Council. The Gospel is so widespread in the world and its message has sunk such deep roots that the great number of beatifications vividly reflects the action of the Holy Spirit and the vitality flowing from Him in the Church's most essential sphere, that of holiness. Indeed, it was the Council that put particular emphasis on the universal call to holiness" (Opening Address to the Extraordinary Consistory in preparation for Jubilee Year 2000, June 13-14, 1994).

He further writes, "The greatest homage which all the Churches can give to Christ on the threshold of the third millennium will be to manifest the Redeemer's all-powerful presence through the fruits of faith, hope and charity present in men and women of many different tongues and races who have followed Christ in the various forms of the Christian vocation" (Pope John Paul II, *Tertio Millennio Adveniente*, no. 37).

✠ There is therefore a whole series of reasons, which can be summed up as follows:

- Saints are made holy by God, and if there are saints, the Church cannot help but recognize and recommend them.
- Vatican Council II spoke of the universal call to holiness.
- The proliferation of local Churches entails the proliferation of models of holiness.
- Holiness is the easiest way to the unity of the Church, and therefore has powerful ecumenical implications.
- We believe, we are reminded by the Apostolic Symbol that we recite at every Mass, that the Church is "one, holy . . . "

How does the Church arrive at canonization?

Church procedure in causes of beatification and canonization was developed over the course of time, its norms continually updated in the light of progress in the historical disciplines, for the sake of agility in the procedure, while still maintaining the integrity of the investigations in a matter of such gravity and importance.

These are the phases:

1. Diocesan phase:

✠ Anyone can ask the bishop of the diocese in which the servant of God died to open a cause of canonization. Saints and holiness are therefore recognized as a bottom-up movement. Even today, it is the Christian people itself that, recognizing through the intuition of the faith the "reputation of holiness," indicates the candidates for canonization to its bishop, who subsequently sends the evidence collected to the appropriate dicastery of the Holy See, the Congregation for the Causes of Saints. A cause cannot be initiated if it has not been shown, through irrefutable evidence, that the servant of God in question is considered a saint or a martyr by a significant portion of the faithful.

✠ The bishop, at the request of the postulator and with the permission of the Holy See, opens the process, normally no earlier than five years after the death of the believer. It is the bishop's responsibility to collect the evidence on the life, the virtues and martyrdom, the alleged miracles, and, if applicable, the ancient devotion to the servant of God whose canonization is being requested. To do this, the bishop enlists the help of various experts who, after examining writings and documents and talking to witnesses, express a judgment on the authenticity and value of these, as well as on the personality of the servant of God.

In particular, the bishop must verify that

- This reputation of holiness or of martyrdom is well-founded, spontaneous (not produced artificially, for example by the mass media), stable, continuous, found among persons upstanding in the faith and in a significant portion of the People of God
- The norms for the diocesan oversight of a cause of beatification and canonization have been applied very carefully
- In the collection of evidence, nothing has been left out that in any way might pertain to the cause, in the certainty that the happy outcome of the cause depends to a great extent on how well it is conducted

✠ If the bishop maintains that the cause has a foundation, he appoints a tribunal (judge, promoter of justice, and notary), which interviews the witnesses and receives from a historical commission all of the documentation on the life, virtues, and reputation of holiness of the servant of God.

2. Pontifical phase:

✠ Once the diocesan investigation has been concluded, all of its findings are sent in duplicate to the Holy See, to the Congregation for Saints in particular, which examines the findings

- Under the formal aspect (to verify whether the findings are valid and authentic)

- Under the aspect of merit (to ascertain whether there is sufficient proof of virtue).

✠ At the conclusion, the aforementioned congregation delivers its assessment of both the virtues and the miracles.

How is the examination of the virtues conducted?

The Congregation for Saints proceeds in this manner:

✠ First comes the preparation of the *Positio*, which is the complete body of procedural and documentational findings, which must be submitted for examination by the specific expert consultants in each field for their judgments on the scientific value of the findings.

✠ The *Positio* (with the written votes of the historical consultants and the further clarifications of the Relator, if necessary) is examined by the theological consultants, who, together with the *Promotor Fidei*, express their judgment of the heroic nature of the virtues of the Servant of God and prepare their own final report, which is submitted along with the *Positio* to the examination of the cardinals and bishops who belong to the Congregation for Saints.

How should "heroic virtue" be understood?

The concept of heroic virtue does not necessarily imply that the actions of the virtuous person are astonishing. "Heroism," explained Cardinal José Saraiva Martins, prefect of the Congregation for Saints, "can quite easily consist in carrying out in an extraordinarily generous and perfect manner one's everyday duties regarding God, one's neighbor, and oneself. Ordinary everyday life is the most common venue for attaining the highest peaks of holiness" (Speech, 2003).

Is a miracle also necessary?

In order to proceed with the beatification of a servant of God, canon law currently requires a miracle obtained through the intercession of the servant of God after his or her death. A miracle is not required for the beatification of a martyr, because martyrdom itself, suffered out of love for God, is an unequivocal sign of the virtuous life of a servant of God.

For canonization, however, another miracle, taking place after beatification, is required for both non-martyrs and martyrs.

Why are miracles required?

✠ There is a historical reason: the Church has always asked for "signs" in confirmation of the virtuous life of a Christian.

✠ Above all, there is a theological reason. Miracles are needed to

- Confirm the doctrine and faith of the servant of God
- Guarantee the judgment of heroic virtue
- Prove that the life of a non-martyr was not secretly *laxior* (less holy) than is attested to by the witnesses

What happens if there are miracles?

✠ The miracle, which St. Thomas defines as "what is done by God outside of the order of nature," is studied under two aspects:

- Scientific: In order to prove that the marvelous occurrence, such as a healing, is unexplainable on the basis of testimony and medical documentation, which means that it exceeds the capacity of nature in regard to the nature of the occurrence itself, the subject, or even just the manner in which it took place
- Theological: In order to verify whether the marvelous occurrence bears the mark of the preternatural, meaning whether it is a real and proper miracle and whether there is a causal connection between the prayers of the servant of God and the marvelous occurrence

✠ It is above all up to the bishop of the diocese where the extraordinary event has taken place to have the miracle studied by a tribunal, which must collect the eyewitness and medical-clinical evidence.

✠ The bishop then sends the findings of the tribunal to the Congregation for the Causes of Saints, which studies them under the procedural profile (to ascertain the validity of the findings) and above all for their merit. To this end

- The findings are first examined separately by two medical experts and then by a joint panel of five physicians, who collect their conclusions (diagnosis, prognosis, therapy, manner of healing unexplainable from a medical point of view, etc.) in a report.

- A *Positio* is then prepared (with all the diocesan findings and the report from the physicians), which is examined by the theologians, who issue a judgment on the preternatural nature of the event
- Finally, this same *Positio*, the report from the physicians, and the judgment of the theologians are submitted to the scrutiny of the cardinals and bishops of the Congregation for Saints, who will evaluate whether the prodigious event is a miracle or not.

✠ The judgment of the cardinals and bishops, on both heroic virtue and the miracle, is submitted by the cardinal prefect of the Congregation for Saints to the pope, who has the exclusive right to declare, with a solemn act, that public ecclesiastical devotion can be bestowed on a Christian with beatification or canonization.

What kind of devotion is due to saints and blesseds?

Saints and blesseds are due a devotion of veneration, not of adoration, which is reserved solely for God.

It must not be forgotten that the ultimate aim of the veneration of the saints is the glory of God and the sanctification of the human person through a life completely conformed to the divine will and the imitation of the virtues of those who were eminent disciples of the Lord.

For more information on this topic, see the following pontifical documents:

Vatican Council II, *Lumen Gentium*, Ch. 5

Pope John Paul II, *Divinus Perfectionis Magister* on the new legislation for the causes of saints, 1983

Congregation for Saints, *Norms to Be Observed in Inquiries Made by Bishops in the Causes of Saints*, 1983; Instruction *Sanctorum Mater*, 2008

Catechism of the Catholic Church, Part Three

Compendium of the CCC, Part Three

II
Angels

Who are the angels?

✠ "The angels are purely spiritual creatures, incorporeal, invisible, immortal, and personal beings endowed with intelligence and will. They ceaselessly contemplate God face-to-face and they glorify him. They serve him and are his messengers in the accomplishment of his saving mission to all" (*Compendium of the* CCC, no. 60).

✠ "With their whole beings the angels are servants and messengers of God. Because they 'always behold the face of my Father who is in heaven' they are 'mighty ones who do his word, hearkening to the voice of his word.' As purely spiritual creatures angels have intelligence and will: they are personal and immortal creatures, surpassing in perfection all visible creatures, as the splendor of their glory bears witness" (CCC, nos. 329-330).

✠ St. Augustine says about them: "The word 'angel' designates the office, not the nature. If one asks for the name of this nature, the answer is that it is spirit; if one asks for the office, the answer is that it is angel: it is spirit for what it is, while for what it does it is angel" (St. Augustine, *Enarratio in Psalmum* 103, 1, 15: CCL 40, 1488).

✠ "Angels, the Gospel says, 'ministered' to Jesus (Mk 1:13); they are the antithesis of Satan. 'Angel' means 'messenger.' . . . We would be removing an important part of the Gospel were we to leave out these beings sent by God, who announce and are a sign of his presence among us. Let us invoke them frequently, so that they may sustain us in our commitment to follow Jesus to the point of identifying with him" (Pope Benedict XVI, *Angelus*, March 1, 2009).

Is the existence of the angels a truth of faith?

Of course. "The existence of the spiritual, non-corporeal beings that Sacred Scripture usually calls 'angels' is a truth of faith. The witness of Scripture is as clear as the unanimity of Tradition" (CCC, no. 328).

What do the angels do in the Old Testament?

✠ The Old Testament describes various interventions of the angels in the life of the people of Israel.

For example:

- The struggle between the angel and Jacob (Gn 32:25-29)
- The ladder climbed by the angels in Jacob's dream (Gn 28:12)

- The three angels who came as guests to Abraham (Gn 18)
- The intervention of the angel who stopped Abraham as he was about to sacrifice Isaac
- The angel who brought the food to the prophet Elijah in the desert

✠ Then there is the compelling invocation of Psalm 148: "Praise the LORD from the heavens; praise him in the heights. Praise him, all you his angels; give praise, all you his hosts . . . Let them all praise the LORD's name; for he commanded and they were created" (Ps 148:1-5).

And what does the New Testament say about the angels?

✠ The New Testament also talks about the angels frequently: See for example

- The angels' proclamation of the Birth of Christ to the shepherds
- The angel who appears to Joseph in a dream, telling him to flee with Mary and the Child
- The angels who worship and serve Jesus after the temptations in the desert
- The angels who proclaim the Resurrection of Christ to Mary Magdalene and the other women
- The liberation of St. Peter from chains and prison in Rome
- The book of Revelation

✠ Especially touching is Jesus' statement about the angels, in defense of the little children: "See that you do not despise one of these little ones, for I say to you that their angels in heaven always look upon the face of my heavenly Father" (Mt 18:10).

What is the relationship between Jesus Christ and the angels?

✠ "Christ is the center of the angelic world. They are his angels: 'When the Son of man comes in his glory, and all the angels with him . . . ' (Mt 25:31).

- They belong to him because they were created through and for him: 'for in him all things were created in heaven and on earth, visible and invisible, whether thrones or dominions or principalities or authorities—all things were created through him and for him' (Col 1:16).
- They belong to him still more because he has made them messengers of his saving plan: 'Are they not all ministering spirits sent to serve, for the sake of those who are to obtain salvation?' (Heb 1:14).

✠ "Angels have been present since creation and throughout the history of salvation, announcing this salvation from afar or near and serving the accomplishment of the divine plan . . .

"From the Incarnation to the Ascension, the life of the Word incarnate is surrounded by the adoration and service of angels. When God 'brings the first-born into the world, he says, "Let all God's angels worship him."' Their song of praise at the birth of Christ has not ceased resounding in the Church's praise: 'Glory to God in the highest!' They protect Jesus in his infancy, serve him in the desert, strengthen him in his agony in the garden, when he could have been saved by them from the hands of his enemies as Israel had been. Again, it is the angels who 'evangelize' by proclaiming the Good News of Christ's Incarnation and Resurrection. They will be present at Christ's return, which they will announce, to serve at his judgment" (CCC, nos. 331-333).

✠ Nonetheless, Jesus is infinitely superior to the angels: He is "as far superior to the angels as the name he has inherited is more excellent than theirs. For to which of the angels did God ever say: 'You are my son; this day I have begotten you'? Or again: 'I will be a father to him, and he shall be a son to me'?" (Heb 1:4-5).

What is meant by the Gospel phrase: "You will see the sky opened and the angels of God ascending and descending on the Son of Man" (Jn 1:51)?

Origen, a priest and theologian who lived between AD 185 and 253, illustrates this phrase as follows:

"The angels descend because Christ had descended first; they were afraid to descend before the Lord of the heavenly powers and of all things (Col 1:16) had ordered it. But when they had seen the Prince of the heavenly hosts dwelling upon the earth, then by this open way they went out after their Lord, obeying the will of the one who established them as guardians of those who believe in his name . . . Because of this, when Christ was born, 'there was a multitude of the heavenly host with the angel, praising God' (Lk 2:12)" (Origen, *Homilies on Ezekiel* I, 7; SC 352, 71-73).

In what way are the angels present in the life of the Church?

"The whole life of the Church benefits from the mysterious and powerful help of angels. In her liturgy, the Church joins with the angels to adore the thrice-holy God. She invokes their assistance (in the funeral liturgy's *In Paradisum deducant te angeli* . . . ['May the angels lead you into Paradise . . . ']). Moreover, in the 'Cherubic Hymn' of the Byzantine Liturgy, she celebrates the memory of certain angels more particularly (St. Michael, St. Gabriel, St. Raphael, and the guardian angels). From its beginning until death, human life is surrounded by their watchful care and intercession" (CCC, nos. 334-336).

"The Church joins with the angels in adoring God, invokes their assistance and commemorates some in her liturgy" (*Compendium of the* CCC, no. 61).

In what way can the faithful, by imitating the angels, worship God?

✠ Worship means rendering devotion to Christ the Lord really present with his Body in the tabernacle. This cult of adoration (or latria) is reserved exclusively for God alone as a term of honor, of recognition of his superiority and our submission.

✠ Eucharistic adoration arises

- From the celebration of the Eucharist. The sacrifice of the Holy Mass is truly the origin and the end of the devotion that is rendered to the Eucharist outside of the Holy Mass, which is therefore intimately connected to the Eucharistic celebration, is its natural prolongation, and is ordered to it.
- From faith in the Real Presence of the Lord. This naturally leads to the external manifestation, public and private, of this same faith.
- From the certainty that the Lord is with us always. "Behold, I am with you always, until the end of the age" (Mt 28:20).

✠ The adoration of the Most Holy Sacrament can be both personal and communal in its various forms, including the exposition of the Most Holy Sacrament, in the monstrance or in the pyx, in prolonged or brief form. This adoration, recommended by the Church to pastors and faithful, is highly expressive of the bond that exists between the celebration of the sacrifice of the Lord (which is in itself the highest act of adoration by the Church) and his permanent presence in the consecrated host.

✠ Adoring Jesus Christ present in the Eucharist outside of Mass, including as reparation, is a consequence of our faith in the mystery celebrated. Adoration is therefore to be understood as preparation for the Holy Mass, as the proper attitude for celebrating the holy mysteries, and as thanksgiving for the gift of the Eucharist.

Are there other ways to adore the Lord?

In addition to the forms of adoration just mentioned, it must be recalled that our love for the Eucharist can be expressed in other ways in which we adore the Lord, such as

- Perpetual adoration, that of the Forty Hours or in other forms, which involve an entire parish, religious community, or Eucharistic association, and provide the opportunity for numerous expressions of Eucharistic devotion
- A simple visit to the Most Holy Sacrament placed in the tabernacle: a brief encounter with Christ suggested by faith in his presence and characterized by silent prayer
- Eucharistic Benediction, which usually concludes Eucharistic processions and adoration when there is a priest or deacon present. Because Benediction of the Most Holy Sacrament is not a complete form of Eucharistic devotion on its own, it must be preceded by a brief exposition, with sufficient time for prayer and silence. It is therefore forbidden to have exposition for the sole purpose of Benediction.
- Eucharistic processions in the streets. These help the faithful to feel like the People of God walking with their Lord, proclaiming faith in God with us and for

us. This is true above all for the Eucharistic procession par excellence, that of *Corpus Domini*. In processions, everything must contribute to emphasizing the dignity of and reverence for the Most Holy Sacrament: the behavior of those present, the decoration of the streets, the ceremonial flowers, the songs and prayers must be a manifestation of faith in the Lord and of praise for him.

- Eucharistic congresses. These, a sign of faith and charity, can be considered a *statio*, or a pause of renewed commitment and prayer to which a community invites the universal Church or a local church invites the other churches of the same region or of the same nation or of the whole world, to explore together some aspect of the Eucharistic mystery and pay it the homage of public veneration.

Who are the archangels?

✠ In the Christian faith, three of the angels are identified as archangels. In the Bible, in fact, and particularly in the book of Tobit, it says that the archangels are those who sit in the presence of God, contemplating his glory and praising him ceaselessly. The Catholic Church recognizes three archangels:

- Michael: Etymologically, his name means "Who is like God?," "greatness of God," "the great God," or "like God." He is the archangel of light and fire; he is the head of the heavenly hosts. He is the one who cast Lucifer out of heaven. Because of this, he is depicted in Christian iconography as a strong, handsome young man wearing armor. He is identified as the protector of the Roman Catholic Church, as well as being the holy patron of the Jewish nation. The liturgy for the deceased invokes him as the companion of souls.

- Gabriel: Etymologically, his name means "power of God," in that it is supposed that he wrestled with Jacob and broke his thigh bone (see Gn 32). He presented himself to Zechariah as "Gabriel, who stand before God" (Lk 1:19). He appeared to the Virgin Mary, announcing the Birth of Jesus to her. Because of this he is considered the patron of ambassadors as well as the angel of Revelation. In Christian iconography, he is depicted as an elegant, majestic young man dressed in sumptuous clothing. He is also frequently depicted on his knees in front of the Blessed Mother with his arms folded over his chest and a scroll, a scepter, or a lily in his hand.
- Raphael: His name means "divine healer," "God heals," or "salvation of God." In the book of Tobit, he accompanies Tobiah on his journey to Mesopotamia to collect his father's money, liberates Sarah from a demon, and makes it possible for her to marry Tobiah. He is often considered the guardian angel par excellence, the head of the guardian angels, the angel of providence who watches over all humanity. He is often depicted, in Christian iconography,

together with the young Tobiah and his dog. He is identified as the protector of pilgrims, meaning those who are making a pilgrimage to a religious place or, even better, are on the journey to God. He is therefore depicted as a wayfarer traveling with staff and sandals, with a flask of water and a sack slung over his shoulder.

✠ The Church celebrates the feast of these three archangels on September 29.

What do the guardian angels do?

✠ We read in the book of Exodus: "See, I am sending an angel before you, to guard you on the way and bring you to the place I have prepared. Be attentive to him and obey him. Do not rebel against him" (Ex 23:20-21).

✠ "Every believer has an angel nearby as protector and shepherd, to guide him to life" (St. Basil the Great, *Adversus Eunomium*, 3, 1: SC 305, 148).

✠ "From its beginning until death, human life is surrounded by their watchful care and intercession" (CCC, no. 336).

✠ We read in the book of Psalms: "For he commands his angels with regard to you, to guard you wherever you go" (Ps 91:11).

St. Bernard comments on this passage of the Bible as follows: "What reverence these words should stir in you, what devotion they should bring to you, what trust they should instill in you! Reverence for the presence, devotion for the benevolence, trust in the protection. They are present, then, and are present to you, not only with you, but also for you. They are present to protect you, they are present to benefit you . . . Let us love the angels of God affectionately, as those who will one day be our co-heirs, while in the meantime they are our guides and tutors, established and ordained for us by the Father . . . They cannot be defeated or seduced, much less can they seduce, these who protect us in all our ways. They are faithful, they are prudent, they are powerful. Why tremble? Let us simply follow them, let us stay close to them and remain in the protection of the God of heaven" (St. Bernard, *Discourse 12 on Psalm 9*, *Opera Omnia*, ed. cisterc. 4 [1996] 458-462).

✠ Devotion to the guardian angels began in the sixteenth century as a separate feast day in many Churches. It was introduced to the Roman calendar in 1615.

What prayers does the Church invite us to address to God through the guardian angels?

✠ On the liturgical Feast of the Guardian Angels (October 2), the Church prays in the Eucharistic celebration like this:

> O God, who in your unfathomable providence are pleased to send your holy Angels to guard us, hear our supplication as we cry to you, that we may always be defended by their protection and rejoice eternally in their company . . .
>
> Receive, O Lord, the offerings we bring before you as we venerate your holy Angels, and graciously grant that

under their constant protection we may be delivered from present dangers and brought happily to life eternal . . .

As you are pleased to nourish us for eternal life with so great a Sacrament, O Lord, direct us by the ministry of Angels into the way of salvation and peace. Through Christ our Lord. (*The Roman Missal*)

✠ Popular Christian tradition has handed down to us this simple but beautiful prayer to the guardian angel:

"Angel of God, my guardian dear, / to whom God's love commits me here, / ever this day be at my side, / to light and guard, to rule and guide. Amen."

✠

For more on this topic:

Catechism of the Catholic Church, nos. 326-336; 350-352; 391-393; 1023-1029

Compendium of the CCC, nos. 59-61

III
Miracles

What is meant by "extraordinary phenomena"?

In this section, when I talk about extraordinary phenomena, I intend to embrace in a single expression everything that belongs, in the religious sphere, to the extraordinary order, meaning that it cannot be understood or explained with human reason alone and cannot be demonstrated scientifically.

✠ I therefore include: apparitions, miracles, revelations, visions . . .

✠ As long as they have taken place after the end of the New Testament period, meaning the end of public Revelation

What is public Revelation?

Public Revelation

- Was accomplished gradually by God beginning with Abraham, and, through the prophets, until the coming of Jesus Christ

- Is witnessed to in the two sections of the Bible: the Old Testament and the New Testament
- Is intended for all people and for the whole person, of every time and place
- Is radically different, in essence and not only in degree, from "private revelations" (which will be examined later)
- Was concluded with Christ in the New Testament, to which the Church feels bound

Why did public Revelation conclude with Christ?

Because Jesus Christ is the mediator and the fullness of Revelation.

"He, being the only-begotten Son of God made man, is the perfect and definitive Word of the Father. In the sending of the Son and the gift of the Spirit, Revelation is now fully complete, although the faith of the Church must gradually grasp its full significance over the course of centuries" (*Compendium of the* CCC, no. 9).

"In times past, God spoke in partial and various ways to our ancestors through the prophets; in these last days, he spoke to us through a son" (Heb 1:1-2).

Christ, the Son of God made man, is therefore the unique, perfect, and definitive Word of the Father, who says and gives everything in him, and there will be no other Word than that.

"From the moment in which he gave us his Son, who is his only and definitive Word, God told us everything once and for all in this Word, and has nothing more to say" (St. John of the Cross).

"The Christian dispensation, therefore, as the new and definitive covenant, will never pass away, and we now await no further new public revelation before the glorious manifestation of our Lord Jesus Christ" (*Dei Verbum*, no. 4).

What are the consequences of this conclusion of public Revelation?

Here are some of them:

✠ The God of the Christians is credible and trustworthy on the basis of Scripture, and not by virtue of messages communicated later to individual believers.

✠ No new manifestation or revelation is to be expected from God, except for the return of Christ, which will inaugurate "new heavens and a new earth" (2 Pt 3:13), allowing God the Father to be "all in all" (1 Cor 15:28).

✠ The Church is bound to the unique event of sacred history and to the Word of the Bible, and its mission is that of guaranteeing, interpreting, exploring, and bearing witness to public Revelation. This takes place through the special assistance of the Holy Spirit, who acts as its guide and leads it to know better and better that treasure that Christ the Lord.

✠ Public Revelation demands our faith: "In it in fact God himself speaks to us through human words and the mediation of the living community of the Church. Faith in God and in his word is different from any other human faith, trust, or opinion. The certainty that it is God who is speaking gives me the assurance that I am in touch with truth itself. It gives me a certitude that is beyond verification by any human way of knowing. It is the certitude upon which I build my life and to which I entrust myself in dying" (Congregation for the Doctrine of the Faith [CDF], *The Message of Fatima*).

✠ Nonetheless, although Revelation has been finalized, it has not yet been made fully explicit. It is the duty of the Christian faith to know it better, to explore it more deeply, to embody it continually, to bear witness to it to all with fidelity and courage. This makes it possible to grasp its full impact gradually, over the course of the centuries.

What are private revelations?

Private revelations

- Are all of those revelations (apparitions, visions, miracles . . .) that take place after the conclusion of the New Testament. They are the apparitions of Jesus, Mary, or the saints, as well as the messages they deliver or the miracles they perform or are performed in their name. All of these extraordinary phenomena (real or presumed) belong to the genre of private revelations. (N.B. In this section, I will always use this expression to indicate and embrace all the extraordinary phenomena that have taken place after the conclusion of public Revelation.)

- Have been recognized, in small numbers, by the authority of the Church, which does not recognize the bulk of them. (For example, according to some calculations there have been more than 1800 individual Marian apparitions; only a dozen of these have official recognition.)
- Do not belong to the deposit of faith, from which the Church draws its certainty about all revealed truths. None of these private revelations (whether approved or not) are part of what Christians are obliged to believe in order to call themselves Christian.

In what way do private revelations make a claim on the faith of the believer?

Private revelations do not make any obligatory claim on the faith of believers, even if they have been officially recognized by the Church. Every believer remains free to decide about them: no Christian is obliged to believe in any private revelation, even if it has been approved by the Church.

In terms of principle, the believer nevertheless should not exclude the possibility that God could intervene in an extraordinary way at any moment, in any place, in any event, with any person. The difficult thing is to discern whether an authentic extraordinary intervention of God has taken place in a particular event.

How do believers deepen their faith?

Vatican Council II indicates three essential ways by which the guidance of the Holy Spirit is realized in the Church and the believer's faith in the Word of God grows. This growth is accomplished

- Through the meditation and study of the believer
- Through the profound intelligence derived from spiritual experience
- Through the preaching of those "who have received through episcopal succession the sure gift of truth" (*Dei Verbum*, no. 8): the pope and the bishops in communion with him

Why is the Church so careful in recognizing private revelations as authentic?

In effect, the Church demonstrates extreme prudence with regard to these phenomena. This prudence is completely justified in that these phenomena could imply that God has forgotten to tell us something in the Sacred Scriptures and that his Revelation in Christ is not unique, total, definitive, concluded.

What is the positive value of private revelations?

Private revelations

- Can help us to understand and live public Revelation more deeply in a specific period of time

- Are truly useful provided that they maintain their strict orientation to Christ and do not become autonomous
- Can reinvigorate the subjective faith of believers, and even of nonbelievers. They are therefore an aid to their faith, as long as they are in keeping with the one public Revelation. They must serve the faith. They must not and cannot add anything to the one definitive public Revelation but can become a humble echoing of it, and sometimes amplify it significantly.
- Inspire new forms of popular devotion, while they deepen and extend the older forms
- Can be a valid aid to understand and live better the Gospel in the present day: an aid that is offered, but the use of which is not obligatory
- Are an aid to understanding the signs of the times, finding the correct Christian response to them

When are private revelations unacceptable?

When they intend or presume to

- Improve, complete, surpass, or correct the definitive public Revelation of Christ
- Be the foundation and origin of faith. The true faith of the believer is not founded on a private revelation, but on the Word of God, on Sacred Scripture, which teaches the truth, having God himself as its author.
- Seek financial gain, taking advantage of people's credulity. For example, what is called "apparition

tourism" must be avoided. We must be careful to prevent the life of faith from being threatened—now as before, or perhaps even more than before—by ideological and economic materialism, and from the unchecked spread of relativism.

What is the main criterion for the authenticity of a private revelation?

The criterion for the truth and value of a private revelation is its strict orientation to Christ himself. When this withdraws from him, when it becomes autonomous or even passes itself off as another and a better plan of salvation, more important than the Gospel, then it certainly no longer comes from the Holy Spirit, who leads us into the Gospel and not out of it.

Whose responsibility is it to discern the authenticity of a private revelation?

It is the responsibility of the living Magisterium of the Church, meaning the successor of Peter, the Bishop of Rome, and the bishops in communion with him, to discern the authenticity of an extraordinary phenomenon. The Magisterium has the duty of serving the Word of God, and, in doing this, enjoys the certain charism of truth.

Guided by the Magisterium of the Church, the sense of the faithful is able to discern and accept what in these private revelations constitutes an authentic appeal of Christ and of his saints to the Church.

The person responsible for the approval of a place as a shrine and of the relative statutes is the local ordinary (see *Code of Canon Law* [CIC], cc. 1230 ff.). It is also the duty of the bishop to make sure that any forms of devotion that are carried out at the shrine correspond to the authentic ecclesial liturgy.

On what criteria does the Church draw in evaluating the authenticity of a private revelation?

✠ These are the fundamental criteria that every bishop is required to follow for the recognition of private revelations: (1) the collection of accurate information about the events, (2) an examination of the message that comes from the apparition and verification that it is not in contrast with the faith, (3) a medical-psychological diagnosis of the visionary, (4) an analysis of the visionary's level of theological education and spiritual advancement, and (5) the study of any miraculous healings strictly connected to the apparitions. If necessary, the local bishop can make use of the help and advice of the episcopal conference and of the Holy See, especially of the CDF.

✠ For the evaluation of a private revelation, three criteria are particularly important:

- First of all, the private revelation must contain a message that, from the point of view of doctrinal content, is absolutely in keeping with Sacred Scripture and with the faith of the Church. And this is not always the case.
- Then the recipient of the apparitions must demonstrate evident signs of psychological maturity, of solid

spirituality, of obedience and fidelity to the Church. The person's sincerity is not necessarily a guarantee of truth. (Visionaries sometimes confuse the communication that they receive with their own ideas. Personal inspiration can overlap with supernatural inspiration, or, sometimes, diabolical inspiration. So great caution is necessary.)

- Finally, the tree is known by the fruits that it manifests, above all during pilgrimages. These fruits are: a spirit of initiative and prayer, conversions, growth in faith, vocations, works of charity . . .

✠ The Church is very prudent and cautious in approving private revelations, above all when the right of public devotion is to be granted, and even more so when it must rule on its supernatural nature. "One of the reasons has to do with the increase in these phenomena, which in all likelihood is due to various causes: the collapse of rationalism, the spasmodic search for mystery, a superficial, insufficiently formed faith, increasing apprehension or anxiety about not knowing what the future will bring . . . It is essential to steer clear of the risk of a 'Church of apparitions,' distrustful of the hierarchy of the Church, as a variant of the well-known opposition of 'charismatic Church—institutional Church'" (Cardinal Tarcisio Bertone, Address, September 21, 2007).

What does it mean that the Church gives its approval to a private revelation?

✠ The Church, through the CDF, approves a private apparition or revelation with the specific formula, *constat de supernaturalitate*. If approval is not given, the formula used is *non constat de supernaturalitate*.

✠ Ecclesial approval of a private revelation contains the following elements:

- The message in question does not contain anything contrary to faith and morals.
- It is permitted to make it public.
- The faithful are authorized to adhere to it in prudent fashion.

✠ Even if no one is obliged to believe in it, the believer should be respectful of private revelations whose authenticity has been recognized by the Church.

What about pilgrimages to the places of private revelations?

About these pilgrimages, a distinction must be made between those that are made to places where private revelations approved by the Church have taken place and those that are not.

✠ If the place has been approved by the Church, it can be visited in either private or public form (with pilgrimages authorized by the ecclesiastical authority).

✠ For the others:

- More attention must be paid to the wise prudence of the Church.
- It would be better not to go there (in part to avoid increasing pseudo-faith and/or commercial activity).
- If one decides to go anyway, one must go there privately, and such pilgrimages must not be considered an authentication of the events that have taken place there.

What is the relationship between private revelations and popular devotion?

"Private revelations often spring from popular piety and leave their stamp on it, giving it a new impulse and opening the way for new forms of it. Nor does this exclude that they will have an effect even on the liturgy, as we see for instance in the feasts of Corpus Christi and of the Sacred Heart of Jesus. From one point of view, the relationship between Revelation and private revelations appears in the relationship between the liturgy and popular piety: the liturgy is the criterion, it is the living form of the Church as a whole, fed directly by the Gospel.

"Popular piety is a sign that the faith is spreading its roots into the heart of a people in such a way that it reaches into daily life. Popular religiosity is the first and fundamental mode of 'inculturation' of the faith. While it must always take its lead and direction from the liturgy, it in turn enriches the faith by involving the heart" (*The Message of Fatima*).

What is the human dimension of private revelations?

It is again Cardinal Joseph Ratzinger who helps us to understand the anthropological structure of private revelations. In this regard, he distinguishes three forms of perception or vision: the physical sense of sight, interior perception, and mystical vision. "It is clear," the cardinal emphasizes, "that in the visions of Lourdes, Fatima and other places it is not a question of normal exterior perception of the senses: the images and forms which are seen are not located spatially, as is the case for example with a tree or a house . . . Therefore we are dealing with the middle category, interior perception. For the visionary, this perception certainly has the force of a presence, equivalent for that person to an external manifestation to the senses."

And he adds, "Interior vision does not mean fantasy . . . The subject, the visionary, is still more powerfully involved. He sees insofar as he is able, in the modes of representation and consciousness available to him. In the case of interior vision, the process of translation is even more extensive than in exterior vision, for the subject shares in an essential way in the formation of the image of what appears. He can arrive at the image only within the bounds of his capacities and possibilities. Such visions therefore are never simple 'photographs' of the other world, but are influenced by the potentialities and limitations of the perceiving subject" (*The Message of Fatima*).

In what situations does God reveal himself today, certainly, in an extraordinary way?

Today as well, God reveals himself in an extraordinary and certain way. For example:

- In the sacraments, which, "instituted by Christ and entrusted to the Church, are efficacious signs of grace perceptible to the senses. Through them divine life is bestowed upon us . . . The sacraments are efficacious *ex opere operato* ('by the very fact that the sacramental action is performed') because it is Christ who acts in the sacraments and communicates the grace they signify. The efficacy of the sacraments does not depend upon the personal holiness of the minister" (*Compendium of the* CCC, nos. 224, 229). In this regard, it must never be forgotten that the miracle that is most widespread and available to all is the one that takes place in our churches when, during the celebration of the Holy Mass, the bread and wine become the Body and Blood of Christ (transubstantiation).
- In the infallible definitions of the Church's Magisterium: "Infallibility is exercised when the Roman Pontiff, in virtue of his office as the Supreme Pastor of the Church, or the College of Bishops, in union

with the Pope especially when joined together in an Ecumenical Council, proclaim by a definitive act a doctrine pertaining to faith or morals. Infallibility is also exercised when the Pope and Bishops in their ordinary Magisterium are in agreement in proposing a doctrine as definitive. Every one of the faithful must adhere to such teaching with the obedience of faith" (*Compendium of the* CCC, no. 185).

✠

For more on this topic, see the following pontifical documents:

Catechism of the Catholic Church, nos. 65-67
Compendium of the CCC, nos. 9-10
Congregation for the Doctrine of the Faith, *The Message of Fatima*, LEV 2000
Code of Canon Law, cc. 1230 ff.

IV
The Devil

Who is the Devil?

✠ The Church teaches that in the beginning, the devils were good angels created by God, but that through their own free and irrevocable choice they became evil, rebellious, rejecting God.

✠ The Gospel of John calls Satan "the ruler of this world" (Jn 12:31). "The devil has sinned from the beginning" (1 Jn 3:8) and personally opposes God and his plan of salvation.

What power does the Devil have over us?

✠ The first Letter of John says, "The whole world is under the power of the evil one" (1 Jn 5:19). St. Paul talks about our battle against the spiritual powers (see Eph 6:10-17). It is also because of him that sin and its consequences (sickness, suffering, cataclysms, and especially death) have entered the world.

✠ The Devil generally operates through temptation and deceit. He is a liar, "the father of lies" (Jn 8:44). He can deceive, lead into error, delude. Just as Jesus is the Truth (see Jn 8:44), so also the Devil is the liar par excellence. The French writer Charles Baudelaire said that the Devil's most cunning trick was convincing the world that he doesn't exist.

✠ The Devil possesses an immense power of seduction:

- He seduced Adam and Eve: of all the works performed by the Devil, "the gravest . . . was the mendacious seduction that led man to disobey God" (CCC, no. 394).
- He even tried to seduce Christ, directly (see Lk 4:1-13) and by using Peter (see Mt 16:23).
- He seeks to seduce the disciples of Christ. The strategy that he follows to achieve this is to convince human beings that a life lived in disobedience to the divine will is better than one lived in obedience. He deceives human beings by persuading them that they do not need God and are self-sufficient, without any need for grace and salvation. He even deceives human beings by diminishing and, in fact, eliminating the sense of sin.

✠ "The power of Satan is, nonetheless, not infinite. He is only a creature, powerful from the fact that he is pure spirit, but still a creature. He cannot prevent the building up of God's reign" (CCC, no. 395).

✠ In addition to being limited, his action "is permitted by divine providence which with strength and gentleness guides human and cosmic history. It is a great mystery that providence should permit diabolical activity, but 'we know that all things work for good for those who love God'" (CCC, no. 395).

Why does God "allow" Satan to "torment" human beings?

Earthly life is a time of trial, during which God allows the Devil to tempt and "test" human beings, but never beyond their strength. We know by faith, however, that God is able to draw great good from this evil, because through his grace the heart emerges purified from the trial, and faith becomes firmer.

How does Jesus behave with demons?

✠ First of all, he talks about the Devil frequently (see for example Mt 4:10; Mk 4:15; Lk 10:18; Jn 8:44).

✠ He also acts against the Devil:

- See the temptation of Jesus in the desert, to which he reacts forcefully (see Lk 4:1-13). "The temptation in the desert shows Jesus, the humble Messiah, who triumphs over Satan by his total adherence to the plan of salvation willed by the Father" (CCC, no. 566).
- In the Gospel of St. Luke, we read that Jesus commands the demons, who recognize him as the Son of God (see Lk 4:41; 8:28 . . .).
- Among the miracles that Jesus performs are liberations from demonic possessions (see Mk 1:25-26; 5:2-20): in realizing these healings, he "took away our infirmities and bore our diseases" (Mt 8:17).

- The Evangelists tell us about several exorcisms by which Jesus liberates people from the torment of the demons, thus anticipating the great victory that he will achieve over the prince of this world (see Mk 1:25-26) with his Death and Resurrection.
- Jesus preaches the coming of the Kingdom of God, which constitutes the defeat of the kingdom of Satan: "If it is by the Spirit of God that I drive out demons, then the kingdom of God has come upon you" (Mt 12:28).
- He also entrusts the power to drive out demons to his Apostles (see Mk 3:15; 6:7, 13; 16:17).
- He overcomes the entire world of evil with his Death and Resurrection. Jesus Christ has conquered Satan and has definitively broken the dominion of the evil spirit (see Col 2:15; Eph 1:21; Rev 12:7-12). He is the "stronger" who has overcome the "strong man" (see Lk 11:21-22). "Take courage," the Lord says, "I have conquered the world" (Jn 16:33).
- Jesus descends to the dead so that "through death he might destroy the one who has the power of death, that is, the devil" (Heb 2:14).

How does one overcome the Devil?

In various, complementary ways:

✠ Above all, with a genuine life of faith—characterized by trustful abandonment to the paternal and provident love of God (see Lk 12:22-31)—and by obedience to his will (see Mt 6:10), in imitation of Christ the Lord. This is the surest defense. The most beautiful victory over the influence of Satan is the constant conversion of our lives, which takes place in a special and continual way in the Sacrament of Reconciliation, through which God frees us from sins committed after our Baptism, restores us to his friendship, and strengthens us with his grace to resist the assaults of the Evil One.

✠ With constant vigilance: "Be sober and vigilant. Your opponent the devil is prowling around like a roaring lion looking for [someone] to devour" (1 Pt 5:8).

✠ By welcoming and bearing witness to the Gospel more and more, with words and works. This requires a complete and courageous proclamation of the Gospel. We must not be afraid of talking about the Devil as well, and above all of the victory that Christ has already achieved over him and continues to achieve in the person of his faithful.

✠ By fighting against his seductions and temptations. "A monumental struggle against the powers of darkness pervades the whole history of man. The battle was joined from the very origins of the world and will continue until the last day, as the Lord has attested. Caught in this conflict, man is obliged to wrestle constantly if he is to cling to what is good. Nor can he achieve his own integrity without valiant efforts and the help of God's grace" (*Gaudium et Spes*, no. 37).

✠ By fleeing from and avoiding sin, which "is an offense against God: 'Against you, you alone, have I sinned, and done that which is evil in your sight.' Sin sets itself against God's love for us and turns our hearts away from it. Like the first sin, it is disobedience, a revolt against God through the will to become 'like gods,' knowing and determining good and evil. Sin is thus 'love of oneself even to contempt of God'" (CCC, no. 1850).

✠ By using discernment. "The Holy Spirit makes us *discern* between trials, which are necessary for the growth of the inner man, and temptation, which leads to sin and death. We must also discern between being tempted and consenting to temptation. Finally, discernment unmasks the lie of temptation, whose object appears to be good, 'pleasing to the eyes' and desirable, when in reality its fruit is death" (CCC, no. 2847).

✠ By praying. "If God is for us, who can be against us?" The Lord himself, in the prayer of the Our Father, has taught us to ask God the Father: "Deliver us from evil." "When we ask to be delivered from the Evil One, we pray as well to be freed from all evils, present, past, and future, of which he is the author or instigator. In this final petition, the Church brings before the Father all the distress of the world. Along with deliverance from the evils that overwhelm humanity, she implores the precious gift of peace and the grace of perseverance in expectation of Christ's return. By praying in this way, she anticipates in humility of faith the gathering together of everyone and everything in him who has 'the keys of Death and Hades,' who 'is and who was and who is to come, the Almighty'" (CCC, no. 2854).

✠ Sometimes even by resorting to exorcism.

What is an exorcism?

✠ Exorcism is an ancient and specific form of prayer that the Church uses against the power of the Devil.

✠ An exorcism takes place when "the Church asks publicly and authoritatively in the name of Jesus Christ that a person or object be protected against the power of the Evil One and withdrawn from his dominion" (CCC, no. 1673).

✠ It is "a prayer in the category of the sacramentals" (*Rite of Exorcism*, Introduction, no. 11). The sacramentals "are sacred signs instituted by the Church to sanctify different circumstances of life. They include a prayer accompanied by the sign of the cross and other signs" (*Compendium of the* CCC, no. 351). Especially significant sacramentals include blessings (of persons, meals, objects, places), consecrations of persons, dedications of things to the worship of God, the blessing of holy oils, and exorcisms.

What are the forms of exorcism?

There are two forms: simple and solemn.

1. The simple/ordinary form of exorcism is practiced during the celebration of Baptism. "Since Baptism signifies liberation from sin and from its instigator the devil, one or more exorcisms are pronounced over the candidate. The celebrant then anoints him with the oil of catechumens, or lays his hands on him, and he explicitly renounces Satan. Thus prepared, he is able to confess the faith of the Church, to which he will be 'entrusted' by Baptism" (CCC, no. 1237).

2. "The solemn exorcism, called 'a major exorcism,' can be performed only by a priest and with the permission of the bishop. The priest must proceed with prudence, strictly observing the rules established by the Church. Exorcism is directed at the expulsion of demons or to the liberation from demonic possession through the spiritual authority which Jesus entrusted to his Church. Illness, especially psychological illness, is a very different matter; treating this is the concern of medical science. Therefore, before an exorcism is performed, it is important to ascertain that one is dealing with the presence of the Evil One, and not an illness" (CCC, no. 1673).

What are the other characteristics of solemn exorcism?

✠ "Exorcism must take place in an atmosphere of faith and of humble, trusting prayer, so that any impression of automatic efficacy may be avoided: liberation from diabolical influence takes place if and when God wills. If, as indicated in number 35 of the introduction, some of the faithful are also present, they should be urged to pray intensely as provided for by the rite.

✠ "In spite of the circumspection with which it is normally celebrated, the rite of exorcism is not a private affair, but an event that concerns the whole community. The exorcist, in fact, is a member of the community; he acts in the name of Christ, and, in the name of the Church, exercises a specific ministry. The believer who asks for exorcism is also a member of the community, one of those members whom the community must love with a preferential love: when he or she is in the power of the Evil One, in fact, he or she is the poorest of the poor, in need of help, understanding, and consolation" (*Rite of Exorcism*, Introduction, nos. 13, 16).

✠ Every act of exorcism is indeed a prayer for the liberation of the possessed person from the evil spirit, but at the same time it is a proclamation of

- The Kingdom of God and of Christ, who bore our infirmities and who, as the only liberator and Savior, delivers us from evil
- Total (spiritual and physical) and mediated (through the Church) liberation from the diabolical influence
- The eschatological reality: a sign that anticipates the final victory of Christ over Satan, over sickness, over death

How does someone become an exorcist?

✠ The exorcist (a term derived from the Greek word *exorkízein*, "to command under oath") is a man of prayer who acts in the name of the Church and by the power of the Holy Spirit. The ministry is a gift from God, conferred by the bishop exclusively upon priests of the diocese, and therefore exercised by them through the Church. Piety, knowledge, integrity of life, balance, discernment, theological preparation, spiritual experience, and capacity of listening are the indispensable prerequisites for a ministry that is also a special journey of holiness, because it leads to direct confrontation with the Devil. The exorcist has a special need for prudence in both verifying the presence of the evil spirit and observing the norms established by the Church.

✠ The ministry of the exorcist, in addition to being one of liberation, is also a ministry of consolation.

Who are the Satanists?

They can be

- Persons with masochistic tendencies, with a need to feel weak in order to then seek out help
- Persons who renounce their personal freedom for the sake of self-pity, passively accepting the orders of important Satanic leaders
- Persons pervaded by a sense of guilt for having committed very serious sins and who are afraid that they will be punished
- Persons who perceive the social-familial-religious environment as tyranny
- Persons who cannot stand law and authority because they are afraid they will be destroyed
- Persons attracted by death: they would like to turn themselves and the world into a cemetery where there is lasting peace
- Persons who use symbols of death: black, funereal curtains in the living room, skulls, hoods, with the sacrifice of animal and sometimes even human victims (from *Toscana oggi*, June 22, 2008)

How is demonic possession recognized?

✠ "The extraordinary demonic phenomena of possession, obsession, harassment, and infestation are possible, but in reality, according to the experts, they are rare" (*Rite of Exorcism*, Preface, no. 7).

✠ The ritual of exorcism points out various criteria and indications that allow one to arrive, with prudent certitude, at the conviction that one is dealing with a demonic possession. It is then that the authorized exorcist can perform the solemn rite of exorcism.

✠ Some of these criteria are

- Speaking or understanding languages previously unknown to the person
- Revealing knowledge of distant or hidden things
- Demonstrating strength beyond the person's own condition
- A vehement aversion to God, the Blessed Mother, the saints, the cross, or sacred images

Are there prayers that can be recited in less serious cases of demonic influence?

Certainly. In the Rite of Exorcism there are also

- Prayers to be recited publicly by a priest, with the permission of the bishop, when it has been prudently determined that there is an influence of Satan over

places, objects, or persons that has not reached the stage of a genuine possession
- A collection of prayers to be recited privately by the faithful when they have reason to suspect that they are subject to demonic influences (see *Rite of Exorcism*, Appendix II, "Prayers of the Faithful for Private Use")

What other helpful guidelines does the Church give about the influence of evil spirits?

Here are some of them:

✠ "Do not seek out the sensation, and avoid both the foolish credulity that sees demonic activity in every anomaly and difficulty, and the preconceived rationalism that excludes a priori any form of activity by evil spirits in the world.

✠ "Be cautious of books, television programs, information in the media that for the sake of profit exploit the widespread interest in unusual or unwholesome phenomena.

✠ "Never consult anyone who practices magic or professes to have occult or mediumistic powers, or claims to have received special powers. In case of any doubt about the presence of demonic influence, it is necessary to turn first of all to the discernment of exorcist priests and to the support and grace offered by the Church, above all in the sacraments.

✠ "Get to know the authentic meaning of the language used by sacred Scripture and by Tradition, and develop a correct attitude toward the presence and action of Satan in the world.

✠ "Remember that superstition, magic, and especially satanism are contrary to the dignity and rationality of the human person and to faith in God the Father almighty and in Jesus Christ our savior" (*Rite of Exorcism*, Preface, no. 8).

✠

For more on this topic:

Rito degli esorcismi, translation of *De exorcismis et supplicationibus quibusdam*, promulgated with a decree from the Congregation for Divine Worship and the Discipline of the Sacraments on November 22, 1998 (the latest edition is from 2004)

Catechism of the Catholic Church, no. 1673

Compendium of the CCC, no. 352

Congregation for the Doctrine of the Faith, *Instruction on Prayers for Healing*, September 14, 2000

V
Magic

What is meant by magical phenomena?

✠ If someone wanted to list all of the superstitions, practices, beliefs, and forms of magic present in the different human cultures, the list would be extremely long. Every thing, being, or event can bring fortune or misfortune, can have positive or negative effects.

Today we are witnessing an astonishing return of magical practices, on account of which the people of today, and especially believers, find themselves facing a real challenge.

✠ It must not be forgotten that all human behavior is always complex and composite, and therefore difficult to decipher in its motivations and expressions.

What kinds of phenomena will be referred to in this section?

The various kinds of phenomena taken into consideration in this section can be summarized as follows:

✠ The many forms of superstition that consist in attributing undue and almost magical importance to certain practices or objects (amulets, horoscope readings, astrology, tarot card readings, lucky or unlucky numbers)

✠ The practices of witchcraft, satanism, and astrology undertaken by healers, fortune-tellers, clairvoyants, mediums, diviners, etc., with which they claim to ally themselves with occult powers and to bend them to their own service or that of others, in order to have special powers both for good (love, money, health) and for evil (curses, spells, black masses)

✠ The different beliefs like reincarnation, relativism, syncretism, esotericism, and spiritism in their various forms (or recourse to the spirits of the dead in order to enter into contact with them and unveil the future or some aspect of it; presumed contact with the deceased through various rites or techniques: séances, mediumship, automatic writing, recordings)

✠ Certain psycho-physical experiences and techniques of concentration and healing that do not of themselves present truths to be believed (e.g., Reiki) but that in reality insinuate a certain vision of the human person and of the world (karma, reincarnation) not in keeping with the Revelation of Jesus Christ

✠ The vast galaxy consisting of the various phenomena of new and old religious movements, which at times, in the common language, are referred to as "sects"

✠ A great number of other attitudes—often taken from Eastern philosophical and religious traditions—that are found in persons who, although they have no intention of adhering to new religious movements, adopt certain ideas or practices that contradict the Christian faith

✠ The various forms of magic

There are various forms of magic?

✠ There is sympathetic magic, according to which like produces like: pouring water on the ground will bring rain, piercing the eyes of a doll will blind or kill the person it represents . . .

✠ There is contagious magic, on the basis of which the "contiguous" acts on the "contiguous," or a part on the whole, in which it is sufficient to bring two animate or inanimate realities into contact with each other in order that a beneficial or harmful force may be transmitted from the one to the other: thus knocking on wood or throwing salt over one's shoulder will keep away negative influences because of the special powers found in these elements.

✠ There is incantatory magic, which attributes special power to symbolic formulas and actions believed to be capable of producing the effects evoked or indicated by them (see Tuscan Episcopal Conference [TEC], A *proposito di magia e di demonologia*, no. 6).

✠ There are white magic and black magic, which tend to seek contact with occult forces that, although considered superior to the individual, can be manipulated and controlled, increasing the power of the sorcerer and his followers. The reason for wanting to acquire magical powers can be material (acquisition of riches or of domination over others) or noble (improvement of oneself and of humanity. In order to attain these ends, a series of intermediate forces will be mobilized: spirits, angels, demons, fluids, energies, powers, etc.).

What is the difference between white magic and black magic?

"Traditionally it has been customary to distinguish between white magic and black magic . . . White magic refers to activities that claim to have beneficial purposes, like the restoration of a love relationship, healing from an illness, the resolution of financial problems, and so on. But this is done through the use of inadequate means, like talismans, amulets, good luck charms, beliefs in combinations of cards, persons, or events, or through recourse to mediumistic practices centered on occult arts or 'superhuman' powers" (Campania Episcopal Conference [CEC], *Io sono il Signore vostro Dio: Nota pastorale a proposito di superstizione, magia, satanismo*, nos. 13-14).

Black magic is even more serious. This directly or indirectly calls upon demonic powers, or in any case claims to act under some influence by them. Black magic is normally performed for evil purposes (to bring illness, disgrace, or psychological disturbance to a rival, to create strong negativity, curses, obstacles, or opposition, to enact revenge, to kill . . .) or to influence the course of events for one's own purposes, especially in order to achieve personal advantages like status and wealth. It is called black magic because of the methods it uses and the ends that it pursues (see TEC, no. 8). This form of magic is a real and proper expression of anti-worship, and its ultimate end is to turn its practitioners into slaves of Satan. It includes the Satanic rites that culminate in black masses.

What are the causes behind the spread of magical practices?

The causes are varied, complex, and complementary:

✠ "Religious ignorance is, without a doubt, the main cause of deviations in this area" (CEC, no. 3). If true faith decreases, superstition increases!

✠ There is "a grave lack of evangelization that does not permit the faithful to adopt a critical attitude toward beliefs and practices that represent only a surrogate of the genuine religious sense, and a sad mystification of the authentic contents of the faith" (TEC, no. 3).

✠ The significant cultural subjectivism that characterizes our time fosters the spread of vague syncretistic beliefs, whereby everyone selects from the various religions or philosophies whatever elements he or she likes. At the same time, it fosters the following of charismatic leaders who promise relief from physical, psychological, or moral disturbances and present themselves as reassuring points of reference.

✠ It must not be forgotten that we live in a fragmented world in which the phenomena of "believing without belonging" or "I believe, my way" are widespread.

✠ The exaltation of the emotional dimension and a widespread sense of anxiety incline people to a highly emotional and magical form of religion and drive them to seek the extraordinary, gratifying experiences and sensations of physical and psychological well-being.

✠ There is also the situation of some religious movements that reject the Church according to the formula "Christ yes, Church no." Others want to replace the Church, affirming "we are the Church."

✠ The existence of such phenomena also indicates that "there are spiritual needs that have not been identified, or that the Church and other religious institutions have not perceived or to which they have been unable to respond. They are a symptom of the state of crisis, especially of fragile persons like young people seeking the absolute or ideals, or adults who are in crisis with regard to their religion or society" (see Cardinal Francis Arinze, *Relazione generale al Concistoro straordinario*).

✠ In particular, we must never forget or underestimate the great influence and constant action of the "father of lies" (Jn 8:44), the Devil, who—as Scripture teaches—tries in every way possible to divert human beings from the truth and lead them into error and evil (see 1 Pt 5:8), in spite of the defeat that he suffered with the coming of the Son of God into the world and the glorious triumph of his Resurrection (see Phil 2:9-11). "An enemy has done this," the householder says to his slaves in the parable of the wheat and the weeds (Mt 13:28). The Devil—as Revelation teaches us—will use his powers and his cleverness until the end of time to deceive the baptized and block the full actualization of God's plan of salvation for the world.

✠ On the other hand, we must be careful in seeing magic as a direct effect—always and in every circumstance—of the Devil. Although the existence and action of the Devil are clearly affirmed by the doctrine of the Church, we must resist the tendency to demonize everything.

✠ The intention in magic is to dominate occult forces, attributing to oneself a superhuman power over creation, over the present, over the future, over others (persons or things), over events, over the deceased. In this way there is an attempt to master God and his power, seeking to replace him. "Magic implies a vision of the world that believes in the existence of occult forces that influence the life of the human person and over which the practitioner (or beneficiary) of magic thinks that he or she exercises control through ritual practices capable of producing effects automatically; recourse to the divinity—when it is present—is merely functional, subordinated to these forces and to the effects desired" (see TEC).

✠ Moreover, there is often a tendency to exploit, intentionally or unintentionally, for profit or not, the credulity and naivety of various persons, taking advantage of the placebo effect. Many practices are the result of money-making scams.

✠ Quite a few people see in these phenomena a religious reawakening or return of the sacred. But this is certainly not a matter of the sacred, much less of the Christian sacred.

✠ Certain phenomena can be produced by paranormal forces, which are natural factors that are little understood and are therefore mistakenly attributed to the realm of the supernatural. In other cases, some phenomena have a completely psychological, psychiatric, neurological, or psychoanalytical explanation.

What are the consequences of the spread of magical practices?

✠ "The Christian faith is adulterated, in that there is an obfuscation of the Lordship of the One Lord who has revealed himself to his people, and the omnipotence of God is emptied of significance, since he is placed beside creatures and 'powers' that take his place and are presented as an alternative to him" (CEC, no. 9).

✠ There is the rejection of a personal and free God, a belief in the existence of occult forces that influence life and over which the practitioner (or beneficiary) of magic thinks that he or she is able to exercise control; recourse to divinity, when it is present, is merely functional, subordinated to these forces and to the effects desired. Magic, in fact, does not acknowledge any power superior to itself; it maintains that it is able to constrain the "spirits" or "demons" evoked to manifest themselves and to do what is required of them. It does not refer to

God, to the personal God of the faith, to his providence over the world, but rather to impersonal occult forces. It maintains that it is able to defend itself from these forces through recourse to spells and amulets, or claims to harness its benefits with formulas of enchantment, potions, or actions connected to the stars, to creation, or to human life.

✠ All of this constitutes a deviation from the religious sense and an attempt to replace God by exercising one's own will for domination and power over events, nature, and one's neighbor, instead of adopting a humble attitude of request and supplication in prayer. There seems to be an echo here of the ancient and familiar voice of the serpent who said to our progenitors, "You will be like gods" (Gn 3:5).

✠ In particular, "black magic represents a very serious sin . . . a deviation from revealed truth . . . contrary to the faith and to the exclusive worship of Christ, the one redeemer and savior of humanity . . . It is in opposition to the true profession of the believer, and is dangerous to salvation" (TEC, no. 12).

What does the Bible say about these practices?

✠ We find clear indications in Sacred Scripture both about the existence of magic and about the types of magical practice: divination (Dt 18:10), witchcraft (Mt 5:11; Na 3:4; Dt 18:10-12), magical art (Wis 17:7), spells (Dt 18:11; Ps 58:6; Eccl 10:11); the use of knots and ties (Ez 13:17-23).

Mention is made of the magic of Jezebel (2 Kgs 9:22); the superstitious practices of King Ahaz (2 Kgs 16:3-4), of

Manasseh (2 Kgs 21:6), and the superstitious practices that Josiah fought against (2 Kgs 23:24).

✠ In Sacred Scripture, the condemnation of magic and of all magical practices is constant and unequivocal:

- Magic and witchcraft (Ex 22:17; Lv 19:26; Dt 18:10; Wis 12:4; Ez 13:18; Acts 19:19; see Acts 13:6-12, 16:16-24; Gal 5:20; Rev 9:21)
- Recourse to necromancers, diviners, casters of spells and charms, under penalty of death (Lev 19:26, 31; 20:6, 27; Dt 18:10-12; Ex 22:17; Rev 21:8; 22:15; Dt 18:10-12; Is 3:1-3; Ex 7:11; Mi 3:5; Na 3:4)

✠ Here are some particularly significant passages:

- Dt 18:10-14: "Let there not be found among you anyone who causes their son or daughter to pass through the fire, or practices divination, or is a soothsayer, augur, or sorcerer, or who casts spells, consults ghosts and spirits, or seeks oracles from the dead. Anyone who does such things is an abomination to the Lord, and because of such abominations the Lord, your God, is dispossessing them before you. You must be altogether sincere with the Lord, your God. Although these nations whom you are about to dispossess listen to their soothsayers and diviners, the Lord, your God, will not permit you to do so."
- Jer 29:8-9: "For thus says the Lord of hosts, the God of Israel: Do not be deceived by the prophets and diviners who are among you; do not listen to those

among you who dream dreams, for they prophesy lies to you in my name; I did not send them—oracle of the Lord."

- Lev 19:26: "Do not recite charms or practice soothsaying."
- Lev 19:31: "Do not turn to ghosts or consult spirits, by which you will be defiled. I, the Lord, am your God."
- See also Lev 20:6, 27; 1 Sm 28:3; 1 Chr 10:13; 2 Kgs 21:6; Is 8:19; Hos 4:12; Jer 2:27; Mt 24:24; Gn 1:14-15; Dt 4:19; Is 47:13; Wis 13:1-5.

What has the Church's attitude been down through the ages?

✠ The Church has always condemned magic and all magical practices in an explicit and incontrovertible way. For example:

- The First Council of Orleans (511) and the Fourth Council of Toledo (633) prohibited the magical use of astrology.
- The constitution of Pius IV *Dominici Gregis Custodiae* (1546) and the encyclical letter of the Holy Office of 1856 warned against the evocation of the souls of the deceased; the 1917 Response of the Holy Office prohibited the attendance of séances.
- See also: the Council of Lyons (1274); the decree *Pro Grecis* of the Council of Florence (1439); the Eleventh Council of Toledo; the Fourth Lateran Council

- In 1942, the Holy Office prohibited the use of the divination pendulum.

✠ In the *Summa Theologica*, St. Thomas Aquinas

- Cites St. Augustine in *De Doctrina Christiana*, Book 2, Chapter 20, where he states that "'anything that involves the consultation of demons or symbolic pacts accepted and concluded with them is superstitious . . . magical talismans, etc.' Divination and the practices mentioned belong to superstition in that they depend on certain actions by demons. And this is why they relate to pacts established with them" (*Summa Theologiae*, II-II, q. 92, a. 2).
- Counts divination among the mortal sins (*Summa Theologiae*, II-II, q. 76, a. 3). "In the Decree, XXVI, q. 5 (canon *Sortes*), it states: 'The lots with which you decide all of your affairs, and which the Fathers have condemned, are nothing other than divination and evil spells. Therefore we wish that they be condemned, and that they no longer be named among Christians: and in order that they may not be practiced, we prohibit them under pain of excommunication'" (*Summa Theologiae*, II-II, q. 76, a. 2).

What does the Church say about spiritualism in particular?

The Church has always condemned any attempt, other than prayer, to establish contact with the souls in the next world

Here are some of the pronouncements in this regard on the part of the Church:

- Pope Sixtus V, with the 1585 constitution *Caeli et Terra Creator*, firmly condemned necromancy and any contact with the spirits of the dead.
- On August 4, 1856, given the explosion of the phenomenon of spiritualism, the Holy Office declared "illicit, heretical, and scandalous the practice of evoking the souls of the dead, receiving responses from them, etc."
- In 1882 (February 1), the Sacred Penitentiary declared it illicit even to attend séances and spiritualist exhibitions.
- In 1886, the Council of Baltimore affirmed the possibility that spiritualism could be connected to demonic activity.
- In 1917 (April 24), responding to another question on the possibility of attending spiritualist exhibitions as a mere observer, Pope Benedict XV reiterated that "it is not licit in any case" to participate in such demonstrations, even if they present themselves as being characterized by an atmosphere of piety and by an explicit intention to have nothing to do with evil spirits.
- The 1905 Catechism of Saint Pius X explains: "All of the practices of spiritualism are illicit, because they are superstitious and often not immune to demonic activity, and thus have been rightly prohibited by the Church."

And what does the *Catechism of the Catholic Church* say in this regard?

✠ In general:

- "The first commandment forbids honoring gods other than the one Lord who has revealed himself to his people. It proscribes superstition and irreligion. Superstition in some sense represents a perverse excess of religion; irreligion is the vice contrary by defect to the virtue of religion" (no. 2110).
- "God's first commandment condemns the main sins of irreligion: tempting God, in words or deeds, sacrilege, and simony" (no. 2118).
- "Tempting God consists in putting his goodness and almighty power to the test by word or deed. Thus Satan tried to induce Jesus to throw himself down from the Temple and, by this gesture, force God to act. Jesus opposed Satan with the word of God: 'You shall not put the LORD your God to the test.' The challenge contained in such tempting of God wounds the respect and trust we owe our Creator and Lord. It always harbors doubt about his love, his providence, and his power" (no. 2119).

✠ In regard to superstition:

"Superstition is the deviation of religious feeling and of the practices this feeling imposes. It can even affect the worship we offer the true God, e.g., when one attributes an importance in some way magical to certain practices otherwise lawful or necessary. To attribute the efficacy of prayers or of sacramental signs to their mere external performance, apart from the interior dispositions that they demand, is to fall into superstition" (no. 2111).

✠ In regard to idolatry:

"The first commandment condemns polytheism. It requires man neither to believe in, nor to venerate, other divinities than the one true God. Scripture constantly recalls this rejection of 'idols [of] silver and gold, the work of men's hands. They have mouths, but do not speak; eyes, but do not see.' These empty idols make their worshipers empty: 'Those who make them are like them; so are all who trust in them.' God, however, is the 'living God' who gives life and intervenes in history" (no. 2112).

"Idolatry not only refers to false pagan worship. It remains a constant temptation to faith. Idolatry consists in divinizing what is not God. Man commits idolatry whenever he honors and reveres a creature in place of God, whether this be gods or demons (for example, satanism), power, pleasure, race, ancestors, the state, money, etc. Jesus says, 'You cannot serve God and mammon.' Many martyrs died for not adoring 'the Beast,' refusing even to simulate such worship. Idolatry rejects the unique Lordship of God; it is therefore incompatible with communion with God" (no. 2113).

"Human life finds its unity in the adoration of the one God. The commandment to worship the Lord alone integrates man and saves him from an endless disintegration. Idolatry is a perversion of man's innate religious sense. An idolater is someone who 'transfers his indestructible notion of God to anything other than God'" (no. 2114).

✠ In regard to divination and magic:

"God can reveal the future to his prophets or to other saints. Still, a sound Christian attitude consists in putting oneself confidently into the hands of Providence for whatever concerns the future, and giving up all unhealthy curiosity about it. Improvidence, however, can constitute a lack of responsibility" (no. 2115).

"All forms of divination are to be rejected: recourse to Satan or demons, conjuring up the dead or other practices falsely supposed to 'unveil' the future. Consulting horoscopes, astrology, palm reading, interpretation of omens and lots, the phenomena of clairvoyance, and recourse to mediums all conceal a desire for power over time, history, and, in the last analysis, other human beings, as well as a wish to conciliate hidden powers. They contradict the honor, respect, and loving fear that we owe to God alone" (no. 2116).

"All practices of magic or sorcery, by which one attempts to tame occult powers, so as to place them at one's service and have a supernatural power over others—even if this were for the sake of restoring their health—are gravely contrary to the virtue of religion. These practices are even more to be condemned when accompanied by the intention of harming someone, or when they have recourse to the intervention of demons. Wearing charms is also reprehensible. Spiritism often implies divination or magical practices; the Church for her part warns the faithful against it. Recourse to so-called traditional cures does not justify either the invocation of evil powers or the exploitation of another's credulity" (no. 2117).

What should we do to eliminate or reduce these unacceptable practices?

The document of the Episcopal Conference of the Marche (ECM), *Disposizioni pastorali circa i fenomeni della superstizione, della magia, e dei nuovi movimenti religiosi*, offers some helpful pastoral guidelines:

✠ "The Church, and the individual communities within it, will perform the work of prevention to the extent to which they return to the heart of Christian life, in its authentic aspects of doctrine and life, catechesis, prayer, the liturgy, charity, and communion."

✠ We must recall the irreplaceable centrality of Jesus Christ: "We the bishops reiterate the absolute and irreplaceable truth according to which the Father has established Christ 'far above every principality, authority, power, and dominion, and every name that is named not only in this age but also in the one to come. And he put all things beneath his feet and gave him as head over all things to the church, which is his body' (Eph 1:21-23). Those who have encountered the Lord Jesus do not need to seek salvation elsewhere.

"Experience teaches us that, in order to stay far away from superstition, magic, spiritualism, and satanism itself, the reminders, reasoning, criticism, and prohibitions of pastors of souls are useless without firm and solid faith in Jesus Christ. Of course, in the face of the dazzling and astonishing promises on the part of the world, the Christian must proclaim Christ, his cross and resurrection. A losing matchup? St. Paul says no. And he does so in the words of Jesus: 'In the world you will have trouble, but take courage, I have conquered the world' (Jn 16:33).

✠ "It is necessary to reaffirm that which is essential to our faith, which is that only the Lord Jesus has defeated the evil one, freeing us from all fear and from the search for magical means to face the difficulties of life."

✠ In order to know Jesus Christ, catechesis is important, especially for young people and adults. "It must assist the faith so that this is not a vague sense of God and of fraternal goodness, but may grow in the awareness of the mystery of Christ, of the Church, and of all the truths of the Catholic faith, so that it is able to judge correctly the events of life and history.

"In this perspective, it is necessary to promote more widely the knowledge of the Bible and of the texts of the Church's magisterium. The liturgy itself is a permanent source to be appreciated for the sake of constant growth in the Christian faith."

✠ We must respond better "to the need for recognition, acceptance, and belonging that is present in the contemporary person marked by solitude and anonymity." This means that Christian communities must constantly seek to be such.

✠ Our communities may truly become "schools of prayer and spiritual life, offering time and space for silence and recollection in order to respond to the widespread desire for interiority. Pastors of souls should give emphasis to listening and to spiritual direction. We must also urge the frequent celebration of the sacrament of Confession and assiduous, fervent participation in the Eucharist."

✠ The Christian must never forget the need to defend himself or herself and to fight against the Devil and all of his works. On November 16, 1972, Paul VI affirmed: "One of the greatest needs today is the defense against that evil which we call demon. A living, spiritual being, perverted and perverting. A terrible reality, mysterious and frightening. Those who refuse to recognize its existence stray from biblical and Church teaching."

✠ In addition to a better understanding of the Catholic faith, a work of prevention is also needed, documenting the techniques and harmful effects of all deceptive proselytism.

✠ In the formation of Christian faith and conscience, pastors of souls must explain that belonging to or even occasionally participating out of curiosity in the groups or movements mentioned is not in keeping with the Catholic faith. "Let there not be found among you anyone who causes their son or daughter to pass through the fire, or practices divination, or is a soothsayer, augur, or sorcerer, or who casts spells, consults ghosts and spirits, or seeks oracles from the dead. Anyone who does such things is an abomination to the LORD, and because of such abominations the LORD, your God, is dispossessing them before you" (Dt 18:10-12). These behaviors are inconsistent with our faith on various levels, even constituting grave matter. It is not rare for them to erupt into genuine pathologies, and they must be confessed in the Sacrament of Reconciliation.

For more on this topic, see the following documents:

Catechism of the Catholic Church, nos. 2110-2117
Compendium of the CCC, no. 445
Tuscan Episcopal Conference (TEC), *A proposito di magia e di demonologia: Nota pastorale* (April 15, 1994)
Campania Episcopal Conference (CEC), *Io sono il Signore vostro Dio: Nota pastorale a proposito di superstizione, magia, satanismo*
Episcopal Conference of the Marche (ECM), *Disposizioni pastorali circa i fenomeni della superstizione, della magia, e dei nuovi movimenti religiosi* (June 3, 2001)
Cardinal Francis Arinze (President of the Pontifical Council for Interreligious Dialogue), *Relazione generale al Concistoro straordinario*, 1991
Archbishop Giuseppe Casale, *Nuova religiosità e nuova evangelizzazione*, pastoral letter of March 6, 1992, Piemme, 1993

VI
Death

What is the origin of death?

"God did not make death" (Wis 1:13) as we undergo it today. It entered the world as a consequence of the first sin of our progenitors, Adam and Eve. It is therefore "the wages of sin" (Rom 6:23). "By the envy of the devil, death entered the world" (Wis 2:24).

What is the meaning of death?

✠ Today there is a tendency to shun and cover up this reality of human life. Just the thought of death causes anguish. By not thinking about it, one has the sense of keeping it away or overcoming it. In reality, death approaches relentlessly, and can come at any moment, at any age, and in any condition.

✠ For every human being, death is

- A sign of the fact that we are human; it belongs to the human condition
- The end of earthly life

- A door that closes one way of living in order to open another; it is not the end of everything
- A reminder of the wisdom of living well the time available to us
- A way of actualizing a fundamental equality among all, beyond social appearances, economic conditions, and cultural capacities

✠ For the Christian, death is illuminated by the Word of God, which offers us a life that illumines and consoles. Death thus becomes

- Something that puts an end to human life as a time open to the acceptance or rejection of the love of God in Christ
- The beginning of eternal life, that new and endless existence that begins after this earthly life
- An encounter with God, Father and Judge
- An opportunity to express an act of obedience and love for the Father, according to the example of Christ

✠ It is precisely because of this Christian vision of death that St. Francis of Assisi was able to exclaim in the Canticle of the Creatures, "Praise to you, my Lord, for our sister bodily death" (*Fonti Francescane*, 263).

What happens in death?

✠ With death comes the separation of the soul and the body. The body of the human person falls into corruption, while the soul, which is immortal, goes to meet God in order to be judged. It will be reunited with its body at the end of time.

✠ "With death, our life-choice becomes definitive—our life stands before the judge" (Pope Benedict XVI, *Spe Salvi*, no. 45).

What does it mean to die in the grace of God?

It means dying with the awareness of not having mortal sin on one's soul. It means dying in peace with God and with one's neighbor. "This saying is trustworthy: If we have died with him we shall also live with him" (2 Tm 2:11).

How is it possible to die with Christ?

It is possible

- By living as children of God during our earthly life
- By frequently asking God to forgive our sins through the Sacrament of Reconciliation (confession)
- By making use, if possible, of the two sacraments instituted by Christ for the seriously ill and for those who are passing from this life to the next: the Sacrament of the Eucharist as Viaticum and the Sacrament of Anointing the Sick

How did Christ overcome death?

By destroying the cause of death, which is sin, with his Death on the Cross and his Resurrection.

How should the condition of the person after death be described?

"One must especially beware of arbitrary imaginative representations: excess of this kind is a major cause of the difficulties that Christian faith often encounters. Respect must however be given to the images employed in the Scriptures. Their profound meaning must be discerned, while avoiding the risk of over-attenuating them, since this often empties of substance the realities designated by the images" (CDF, *Letter on Certain Questions Concerning Eschatology*).

What happens after death?

The soul, separated from the body, is judged by God on the basis of its faith and works. This is the particular judgment by which each one is given immediate retribution for his or her earthly life.

✠ This retribution consists in

- Admission into the eternal joy of heaven
  - Immediately after death
  - After adequate purification (Purgatory)
- Or eternal damnation in hell

What is heaven?

Heaven is the state of full and definitive happiness. This happiness consists in seeing God "as he is" (1 Jn 3:2), "face to face" (1 Cor 13:12). God will then be known and loved as the highest, supreme happiness of the human person, the ultimate end and the full realization of the person's deepest aspirations. Heaven therefore consists in living the Trinitarian life: being, for all eternity, with God, through Christ, in the Holy Spirit.

This mystery of the beatific vision, of blessed communion with God and with all those who are in Christ, surpasses any possibility of understanding and description. It cannot be localized, just as God cannot be localized. Sacred Scripture speaks of it in images: life, light, peace, wedding banquet, house of the Father, heavenly Jerusalem . . .

What is Purgatory?

Purgatory is the purification of those who die in the grace of God and therefore are already certain to enter heaven but need further purification in order to attain the holiness necessary to enter into the joy of heaven.

How can we assist this purification?

✠ God purifies, with the merits of Christ's Death and Resurrection, those who are in Purgatory, making use also of the help that we are able to give them.

✠ We, who are still pilgrims here on earth, can in fact help our deceased who are in Purgatory with

- Our prayers of suffrage, in particular by participating in the celebration of the Holy Mass for them
- Works of penance and charity

- Indulgences, which are the remission granted by God for the temporal punishment due for sins already forgiven in terms of guilt. Every Christian, a pilgrim on this earth, can acquire, through the intervention of the Church, these indulgences, if he or she is properly disposed and under specific conditions, and can apply them to the deceased in such a way that they may be unburdened from the temporal punishments due for their sins.

What is hell?

✠ Hell is the eternal damnation of those who, by their own free choice, die in mortal sin without having repented and without accepting the merciful love of God. Jesus expresses this reality in a few images: Gehenna, inextinguishable fire, burning furnace . . . These are images that describe the state of extreme suffering, of eternal damnation, that afflicts those who are in hell.

✠ The main punishment of hell consists in eternal separation from God. Only in him, in fact, can human beings have life and happiness, for which they were created and to which they aspire.

✠ God does not predestine anyone to go to hell. On the contrary, he, as the good Father, wants all to be saved and to arrive at his House: heaven. This is why he sent his Son to die and rise again. He does not wish "that any should perish but that all should come to repentance" (2 Pt 3:9). This is why he reprimands every single person during his or her earthly life, both gently and sometimes sternly (as every good father does with his child). And yet, having created the human person free, God respects the decisions of the person, above all at the crucial moment of death. Thus it is the human person himself who, in full freedom and responsibility, excludes himself from heaven, and, persisting in a radical rejection of God, deserves hell.

What is the final and universal judgment?

It is the judgment that God will issue at the end of time, at the end of the world, when Christ "comes in his glory, and all the angels with him . . . and all the nations will be assembled before him. And he will separate them one from another . . . and these will go off to eternal punishment, but the righteous to eternal life" (Mt 25:31-46).

With this judgment

✠ All of the bodies of human beings will rise again. Every body, transformed from corruptible and mortal into incorruptible and eternal, will be united with its soul, sharing with it the condition of heaven or of hell: the condition of the soul since the moment of bodily death.

✠ Among all of the saints of heaven there will be a fraternal communion that is "extremely delicious, because each will have all the benefits of all the other Blessed. Everyone will love the other as himself, and thus will enjoy the good of the other as his own. So the greater the joy of all the Blessed, the greater the joy of each one" (St. Thomas Aquinas, *Conference on the Creed*).

✠ There will be "new heavens and a new earth" (2 Pt 3:13). The present universe, freed from all slavery, will be a new universe, in which there will be "no more death or mourning, wailing or pain, [for] the old order has passed away" (Rev 21:4).

✠ There will be the complete and definitive fulfillment of the plan of God to "sum up all things in Christ, in heaven and on earth" (Eph 1:10). God will be "all in all" (1 Cor 15:28).

When will the last judgment take place?

Only God knows the day and the hour of this definitive event. We know only that it will take place "on the last day" (Jn 6:36), at the end of this world.

What is the basis of our faith in the resurrection of the body?

✠ Faith in God, who "is not God of the dead but of the living" (Mk 12:27)

✠ Jesus Christ, who

- Said, "I am the resurrection and the life" (Jn 11:25)
- Worked several "resurrections" during his earthly life: of Lazarus, of the son of the widow of Nain, of the daughter of Jairus. These "resurrections," which were a return to the previous life, were signs of his being "the Resurrection," and prefigurations of his rising.

- Made this solemn promise before dying: "In my Father's house there are many dwelling places. If there were not, would I have told you that I am going to prepare a place for you? And if I go and prepare a place for you, I will come back again and take you to myself, so that where I am you also may be" (Jn 14:2-3).
- Freely underwent death, and death on the Cross, for our salvation. With his Death he defeated death, for himself and for all of us.
- Rose with his own Body, transformed and glorified. "If Christ has not been raised, then empty [too] is our preaching; empty, too, your faith" (1 Cor 15:14).
- Is the principle, foundation, and certainty of our resurrection as well. He is "the firstborn from the dead" (Col 1:18); "God raised the Lord and will also raise us by his power" (1 Cor 6:13).

How will the resurrection of our bodies take place?

To know the way in which the resurrection will take place exceeds the capacity of our intellect. It is accessible only in the faith. "Why do people find it so hard to believe that they will live with God one day, when something much more incredible has already happened, that God died for humanity?" (St. Augustine, *Disc. Guelf.*, 3).

What is the difference between the resurrection of the body and reincarnation?

There is an enormous difference between the two, in that

- The resurrection is not a return to the previous life but is a new existence with a completely transformed body
- Every life is unique and unrepeatable
- "It is appointed that human beings die once" (Heb 9:27)

In what sense does the Christian die and rise every day?

Every day of life here on earth is for the Christian a participation in the Death and Resurrection of Christ, from two points of view:

- Sacramental: In the Sacrament of Baptism, we die with Christ to sin (we are liberated from sin by him) and we rise to new life, to the life of adopted children of God, members of Christ and of his Church, temples of the Holy Spirit.
- Moral: Every day we are called to flee from sin, to avoid it, to repent and rise again from it, in order to live every moment with joy, as children of God, seeking "what is above, where Christ is seated at the right hand of God" (Col 3:1).

✠

For more on this topic, see the following pontifical documents:

Catechism of the Catholic Church, nos. 988-1060
Compendium of the CCC, nos. 202-216
Congregation for the Doctrine of the Faith, *Letter on Certain Questions Concerning Eschatology*, 1979

VII
Hope

Presented here are some aspects of the encyclical by the Holy Father Benedict XVI *Spe salvi* [*facti sumus*]—"In hope we were saved" (Rom 8:24).

What is Christian hope?

Hope is the Christian virtue by which we expect to enjoy, when we die in the grace of God, full and eternal happiness, which is God himself (see *Compendium of the* CCC, nos. 207-216, 387).

True hope, therefore, is not something, but Someone. It is not based on things that pass away and can be taken away, but on God, who gives himself forever. "This great hope can only be God, who encompasses the whole of reality and who can bestow upon us what we, by ourselves, cannot attain. The fact that it comes to us as a gift is actually part of hope. God is the foundation of hope: not any god, but the God who has a human face and who has loved us to the end, each one of us and humanity in its entirety" (*Spe Salvi*, no. 31).

What questions does hope answer?

✠ The fundamental and existential questions that arise in the heart of every person, such as: How can we live? How is it possible to "face our present" (*Spe Salvi*, no. 1), so often marked by confusion and pain? How can we bear the effort of living every day? What remains when everything passes away?

✠ The human person nurtures many hopes during his life. When some or all of them come true, he becomes aware of desiring even more, in that he is not yet fully satisfied. He intuits that "only something infinite will suffice for him, something that will always be more than he can ever attain" (*Spe Salvi*, no. 30).

What are the characteristics of hope?

Christian hope

- Is a distinctive element of Christians. Through hope "they have a future: it is not that they know the details of what awaits them, but they know in general terms that their life will not end in emptiness" (*Spe Salvi*, no. 2).
- "Is preceded by the expectation which God cultivates in our regard! Yes, God loves us and for this very reason expects that we return to him, that we open our hearts to his love, that we place our hands in his and remember that we are his children. This attitude of God always precedes our hope, exactly as his love always reaches us first" (Pope Benedict XVI, Homily

at Vespers of the First Sunday of Advent, December 1, 2007).

- Is referred to as a theological virtue in that God is its source, its support, and its end
- Is not only informative, but performative, which means that Christian hope "is not merely a communication of things that can be known—it is one that makes things happen and is life-changing" (*Spe Salvi*, no. 3)
- Is stronger than suffering and slavery, and because of this transforms life and the world from the inside (see *Spe Salvi*, no. 4)
- "Is always essentially also hope for others; only thus is it truly hope for me too. As Christians we should never limit ourselves to asking: How can I save myself? We should also ask: What can I do in order that others may be saved" (*Spe Salvi*, no. 48). Salvation "has always been considered a 'social' reality" (*Spe Salvi*, no. 14). "To live for him [Christ] means allowing oneself to be drawn into his *being for others*" (*Spe Salvi*, no. 28).

What is the source of hope?

Hope comes from the encounter with Jesus Christ, who

- Allows us to "know God—the true God—[which] means to receive hope" (*Spe Salvi*, no. 3), to discover God as good and merciful Father, that God-Love whom Jesus has revealed to us with his Incarnation, with his earthly life and his preaching, and above all with his Death and Resurrection. True and sure hope is founded on faith in God-Love, as the merciful Father who "so loved the world that he gave his only Son" (Jn 3:16). Christian hope is therefore the equivalent of faith, in the sense that

- "Faith is the realization of what is hoped for and evidence of things not seen" (Heb 11:1). "Faith is the substance of hope" (*Spe Salvi*, no. 10).
- "The present-day crisis of faith . . . is essentially a crisis of Christian hope" (*Spe Salvi*, no. 17)

■ Makes us truly free. Christ "tells us who man truly is and what a man must do in order to be truly human . . . He also shows us the way beyond death" (*Spe Salvi*, no. 6).

■ "Has already communicated to us the 'substance' of things to come, and thus the expectation of God acquires a new certainty. It is the expectation of things to come from the perspective of a present that is already given. It is a looking-forward in Christ's presence, with Christ who is present, to the perfecting of his Body, to his definitive coming" (*Spe Salvi*, no. 9).

■ Gives us eternal life

What is eternal life?

"This is eternal life, that they should know you, the only true God, and the one whom you sent, Jesus Christ" (Jn 17:3). "If we are in relation with him who does not die, who is Life itself and Love itself, then we are in life. Then we 'live'" (*Spe Salvi*, no. 27), and we live forever.

To what is Christian hope opposed?

✠ The atheism of the nineteenth and twentieth centuries, which involved "a protest against the injustices of the world," but became a "protest against God." Nonetheless, "if in the face of this world's suffering, protest against God is understandable, the claim that humanity can and must do what no God actually does or is able to do is both presumptuous and intrinsically false. It is no accident that this idea has led to the greatest forms of cruelty and violations of justice; rather, it is grounded in the intrinsic falsity of the claim" (*Spe Salvi*, no. 42).

✠ Marxism, the teachings of which on the dictatorship of the proletariat have left behind "a trail of appalling destruction." "He forgot man and he forgot man's freedom . . . He thought that once the economy had been put right, everything would automatically be put right. His real error is materialism: man, in fact, is not merely the product of economic conditions, and it is not possible to redeem him purely from the outside by creating a favorable economic environment" (*Spe Salvi*, nos. 20-21).

✠ The myth of progress, understood "as the new form of human hope" (*Spe Salvi*, no. 20), as "a greater and greater mastery over nature," which brings the illusory belief that the human person can be redeemed through science, and has confined faith and hope increasingly to the private and individual sphere.

In order to eliminate "the ambiguity of progress"—an ambiguity due to the fact that it "offers new possibilities for good, but it also opens up appalling possibilities for evil" (*Spe Salvi*, no. 22)—it is necessary that

- There be a growth of the inner person, a moral growth of humanity. "If technical progress is not matched by corresponding progress in man's ethical formation, in man's inner growth (see Eph 3:16; 2 Cor 4:16), then it is not progress at all, but a threat for man and for the world" (*Spe Salvi*, no. 22).
- Reason, "God's great gift to man," must open itself to faith. It cannot, in fact, forget that "the victory of reason over unreason is also a goal of the Christian life" (*Spe Salvi*, nos. 22-23).

"Science can contribute greatly to making the world and mankind more human . . . It is not science that redeems man: man is redeemed by love . . . The human being needs unconditional love. He needs the certainty which makes him say: 'Neither death, nor life, nor angels, nor principalities, nor things present, nor things to come, nor powers, nor height, nor depth, nor anything else in all creation, will be able to separate us from the love of God in Christ Jesus our Lord' (Rom 8:38-39). If this absolute love exists, with its absolute certainty, then—only then—is man 'redeemed,' whatever should happen to him in his particular circumstances. This is what it means to say: Jesus Christ has 'redeemed' us" (*Spe Salvi*, nos. 24-26).

✠ Materialism: "It is not the elemental spirits of the universe, the laws of matter, which ultimately govern the world and mankind, but a personal God governs the stars, that is, the universe; it is not the laws of matter and of evolution that have the final say, but reason, will, love—a Person . . . Life is not a simple product of laws and the randomness of matter" (*Spe Salvi*, no. 5).

✠ "The contemporary nihilism that corrodes the hope in man's heart, inducing him to think that within and around him nothingness prevails: nothing before birth and nothing after death. In fact, if God is lacking, hope is lacking. Everything loses its 'substance.' It is as if the dimension of depth were missing and everything were flattened out and deprived of its symbolic relief, its 'projection' in comparison with mere materiality" (Pope Benedict XVI, Homily at Vespers of the First Sunday of Advent, December 1, 2007).

✠ The confusion and anguish of today, which can be summed up in the words of an ancient epitaph of the first centuries of Christianity: "*In nihil ab nihilo quam cito recidimus* (How quickly we fall back from nothing to nothing)" (*Spe Salvi*, no. 2).

✠ A certain kind of Christian modernism that "has to a large extent restricted its attention to the individual and his salvation" (*Spe Salvi*, no. 25); in which "Biblical hope in the Kingdom of God has been displaced by hope in the kingdom of man, the hope of a better world which would be the real 'Kingdom of God.' . . . Hence, while we must always be committed to the improvement of the world, tomorrow's better world cannot be the proper and sufficient content of our hope. And in this regard the question always arises: When is the world 'better'? What makes it good? By what standard are we to judge its goodness? What are the paths that lead to this 'goodness'?" (*Spe Salvi*, no. 30).

How is hope learned and exercised?

There are four main ways:

1. *Prayer*.

- "When no one listens to me any more, God still listens to me. When I can no longer talk to anyone or call upon anyone, I can always talk to God. When there is no longer anyone to help me deal with a need or expectation that goes beyond the human capacity for hope, he can help me" (*Spe Salvi*, no. 32).
- Prayer "must on the one hand be something very personal, an encounter between my intimate self and God, the living God. On the other hand it must be constantly guided and enlightened by the great prayers of the Church and of the saints, by liturgical prayer . . . Praying must always involve this intermingling of public and personal prayer" (*Spe Salvi*, no. 34).

2. *Action*. Hope in the Christian sense "is hope in action," as "we work towards a brighter and more humane world . . . Certainly we cannot 'build' the Kingdom of God by our own efforts—what we build will always be the kingdom of man with all the limitations proper to our human nature. The Kingdom of God is a gift, and precisely because of this, it is great and beautiful, and constitutes the response to our hope . . . However, even when we are fully aware that Heaven far exceeds what we can merit, it will always be true that our

behavior is not indifferent before God and therefore is not indifferent for the unfolding of history. We can open ourselves and the world and allow God to enter: we can open ourselves to truth, to love, to what is good . . . So on the one hand, our actions engender hope for us and for others; but at the same time, it is the great hope based upon God's promises that gives us courage and directs our action in good times and bad" (*Spe Salvi*, no. 35).

3. *Suffering*. This is the other way in which hope is learned: "Certainly we must do whatever we can to reduce suffering," however "it is not by sidestepping or fleeing from suffering that we are healed, but rather by our capacity for accepting it, maturing through it and finding meaning through union with Christ, who suffered with infinite love" (*Spe Salvi*, nos. 36-37) (see the section "Illness").

4. *The judgment of God*. "Faith in the Last Judgment is first and foremost hope . . . The image of the Last Judgment is not primarily an image of terror, but an image of hope; for us it may even be the decisive image of hope . . . The judgment of God is hope, both because it is justice and because it is grace. If it were merely grace, making all earthly things cease to matter, God would still owe us an answer to the question about justice—the crucial question that we ask of history and of God. If it were merely justice, in the end it could bring only fear to us all" (*Spe Salvi*, nos. 43, 44, 47). "Both these things—justice and grace—must be seen in their correct inner relationship. Grace does not cancel out justice. It does not make wrong into right. It is not a sponge which wipes everything away, so that whatever someone has done on earth ends up being of equal value" (*Spe Salvi*, no. 44).

What does hope say about the ultimate realities?

Christians are waiting for the ultimate realities, once called the "last things": death, judgment, heaven, and hell (see the section "Death").

What images are used to express hope?

✠ The image of hope most cherished by the Christian tradition are those of the Gospels, and three in particular:

- The humble silent waiting of Israel, as exemplified by the elderly Simeon and the prophetess Anna (see Lk 2:22-40)
- The figure of the Good Shepherd, which was very dear to the primitive Church: "There the shepherd was generally an expression of the dream of a tranquil and simple life, for which the people, amid the confusion of the big cities, felt a certain longing. Now the image was read as part of a new scenario which gave it a deeper content: 'The Lord is my shepherd: I shall not want . . . Even though I walk through the valley of the shadow of death, I fear no evil, because you are with me . . .' (Ps 23[22]:1, 4). The true shepherd is one who knows even the path that passes through the valley of death; one who walks with me even on the path of final solitude, where no one can accompany me, guiding me through: he himself has walked this path, he has descended into the kingdom of death, he has conquered death, and he has returned to accompany us now and to give us the certainty

that, together with him, we can find a way through. The realization that there is One who even in death accompanies me, and with his 'rod and his staff comforts me,' so that 'I fear no evil' (cf. Ps 23[22]:4)—this was the new 'hope' that arose over the life of believers" (*Spe Salvi*, no. 6).

- The expectant Mary, on her way to visit Elizabeth and hastening over the mountains of Judea: "The image of the Church to come, which carries the hope of the world in her womb across the mountains of history" (*Spe Salvi*, no. 50).

✠ "Towards the end of the third century, on the sarcophagus of a child in Rome, we find for the first time, in the context of the resurrection of Lazarus, the figure of Christ as the true philosopher, holding the Gospel in one hand and the philosopher's traveling staff in the other. With his staff, he conquers death; the Gospel brings the truth that itinerant philosophers had searched for in vain. In this image, which then became a common feature of sarcophagus art for a long time, we see clearly what both educated and simple people found in Christ: he tells us who man truly is and what a man must do in order to be truly human. He shows us the way, and this way is the truth. He himself is both the way and the truth, and therefore he is also the life which all of us are seeking. He also shows us the way beyond death; only someone able to do this is a true teacher of life" (*Spe Salvi*, no. 6).

What saints does the pope cite as models of hope?

Among the myriads of women and men who have given the ultimate witness to the name of the Lord, but also in the pain and joy of every day, in "minor daily hardships," Pope Benedict XVI recalls in particular

✠ The life of an African slave, St. Josephine Bakhita, born in 1869 in Darfur in Sudan, who finally recognized God not as a terrible "master," but as someone "totally different" who changed her life. She used to say, "I am definitively loved and whatever happens to me, I am awaited by this Love" (*Spe Salvi*, no. 3).

✠ The harrowing testimony, preserved in a genuine "letter from hell," of the Vietnamese martyr Paul Le-Bao-Tinh († 1857). Even in the abyss of prison and of the hatred unleashed in the victims themselves, this "prisoner for the name of Christ" experienced salvation in hope (see *Spe Salvi*, no. 37).

✠ The Vietnamese cardinal Francis Xavier Nguyen Van Thuan († 2002), in prison for thirteen years, nine of them in isolation, who said that in a situation of apparently complete desperation, listening to God and being able to talk to him became an increasingly powerful source of hope (see *Spe Salvi*, no. 32)

Who is the star of hope?

Mary Most Holy!

"With a hymn composed in the eighth or ninth century, thus for over a thousand years, the Church has greeted

Mary, the Mother of God, as 'Star of the Sea': *Ave maris stella*. Human life is a journey. Towards what destination? How do we find the way? Life is like a voyage on the sea of history, often dark and stormy, a voyage in which we watch for the stars that indicate the route. The true stars of our life are the people who have lived good lives. They are lights of hope. Certainly, Jesus Christ is the true light, the sun that has risen above all the shadows of history. But to reach him we also need lights close by—people who shine with his light and so guide us along our way. Who more than Mary could be a star of hope for us? With her 'yes' she opened the door of our world to God himself; she became the living Ark of the Covenant, in whom God took flesh, became one of us, and pitched his tent among us (cf. Jn 1:14) . . . Holy Mary, Mother of God, our Mother, teach us to believe, to hope, to love with you. Show us the way to his Kingdom! Star of the Sea, shine upon us and guide us on our way!" (*Spe Salvi*, nos. 49-50).

✠

For more on this topic, see the following pontifical documents:

Pope Benedict XVI, *Spe Salvi*
Catechism of the Catholic Church, 1020-1060; 1817-1821
Compendium of the CCC, nos. 207-216; 38

VIII
Illness

What is the origin of illness?

✠ The Christian faith affirms that God did not create illness. It entered the world because of the first sin committed by Adam and Eve, when, tempted by the Devil and abusing their freedom, they disobeyed God. They wanted to be superior to God himself and were eager to pursue their ends apart from God. After this, the sins of every single person would do nothing but expand the world of human suffering.

✠ God, therefore, does not want illness; he did not create evil and death. But from the moment in which these, on account of sin, entered the world, his love has been entirely extended to restoring human beings, to healing them from sin and from every evil and filling them with life, peace, and joy. This is why he sent his Son Jesus, who died and rose in order to free human beings from sin and its consequences.

What is the meaning of illness?

✠ Illness, which touches everyone sooner or later and involves the person on all levels (from the physical to the psychological, spiritual, and moral), is and remains forever a mystery, an enigma.

✠ Science and technology can help us to find a response to illness. They can treat it, alleviate it, eliminate it at least in part, but they will never be able to eliminate it entirely, and above all they will never be able to give a satisfactory answer to the fundamental questions that suffering, illness, and death itself raise within the human heart.

✠ The meaning of illness, of pain, and of suffering must be explored while also taking into account their medical, scientific, historical, philosophical, biblical, and theological foundations.

✠ It is especially important to explore the texts of Sacred Scripture on the vision of suffering, on the meaning of death.

✠ The ultimate meaning of these realities can be discovered only in the light of the Christian faith: "Through Christ and in Christ, the riddles of sorrow and death grow meaningful. Apart from His gospel, they overwhelm us" (*Gaudium et Spes*, no. 22).

✠ God, in fact, did not spare from suffering and even death his own divine Son Jesus, who overcame sin and its effects (illness, suffering, violence, and death) with his Death on the Cross, and above all with his Resurrection.

✠ And Christ achieves this victory first of all for himself, destroying death with his Resurrection, and then also for us. In fact, through the Baptism that he instituted, we are forgiven of Original Sin, and we rise to the life of the children of God. Then, during the course of our life here on earth, fighting against sin and its consequences, we achieve together with Christ our own victory, which for now is partial, waiting for the definitive victory that Christ will realize for us at the end of this world, when he will destroy all suffering, illness, and death.

✠ Therefore, suffering can become a serene abandonment to the divine will and a participation in the sacrifice of Christ.

Why do illness and suffering continue to exist despite the fact that God is good, omnipotent, provident?

✠ "How is it possible to perceive the merciful love of God, who never abandons his children in trial, even in these difficult situations? Such questions are frequent and at times disturbing. Truly, they find no adequate answers on the merely human level since the meaning of pain, illness and death remains incomprehensible to the human mind. However, the light of faith comes to our aid. The Word of God reveals to us that even these ills are mysteriously 'embraced' by the divine plan of salvation; faith helps us to consider human life beautiful and worthy of living to the full, even when it is undermined by evil. God created the human being for happiness and for life, while illness and death entered the world as a consequence of sin. However, the Lord has not left us to ourselves. He, the Father of life, is the physician of man par excellence who ever lovingly bends over suffering humanity" (Pope Benedict XVI, Homily, 17th World Day of the Sick, February 11, 2009).

✠ The *Catechism of the Catholic Church* states in this regard:

"To this question, as pressing as it is unavoidable and as painful as it is mysterious, no quick answer will suffice. Only Christian faith as a whole constitutes the answer to this question: the goodness of creation, the drama of sin and the patient love of God who comes to meet man by his covenants, the redemptive Incarnation of his Son, his gift of the Spirit, his gathering of the Church, the power of the sacraments and his call to a blessed life to which free creatures are invited to consent in advance, but from which, by a terrible mystery, they can also turn away in advance. There is not a single aspect of the Christian message that is not in part an answer to the question of evil.

"But why did God not create a world so perfect that no evil could exist in it? With infinite power God could always create something better. But with infinite wisdom and goodness God freely willed to create a world 'in a state of journeying' towards its ultimate perfection. In God's plan this process of becoming involves the appearance of certain beings and the disappearance of others, the existence of the more perfect alongside the less perfect, both constructive and destructive forces of nature. With physical good there exists also physical evil as long as creation has not reached perfection . . .

"In time we can discover that God in his almighty providence can bring a good from the consequences of an evil, even a moral evil, caused by his creatures . . . From the greatest moral evil ever committed—the rejection and murder of God's only Son, caused by the sins of all men—God, by his grace that 'overflowed all the more,' brought the greatest of goods: the glorification of Christ and our redemption. But for all that, evil never becomes a good . . .

"We firmly believe that God is master of the world and of its history. But the ways of his providence are often unknown to us. Only at the end, when our partial knowledge ceases, when we see God 'face to face,' will we fully know the ways by which—even through the dramas of evil and sin—God has guided his creation to that definitive sabbath rest for which he created heaven and earth" (CCC, nos. 309, 310, 312, 314).

✠ It must not be forgotten that God did not spare even his Son, Jesus Christ, from suffering. And yet Christ was and is, in an absolute sense, the most innocent and the most worthy.

How did Christ behave toward the sick?

✠ During his earthly life, Christ had a special preference for the sick and the suffering. In fact:

- He had a preference for those who suffer.
- He healed many of the sick who came to him with trust. These healings demonstrate that Jesus is truly "God who saves."
- Nonetheless he did not come to eliminate all evils here below, but to liberate human beings from the most serious form of slavery: that of sin, which is the cause of all evil and suffering.

- He identified himself with the sick: "I was ill and you visited me" (see Mt 25:36); "He took away our infirmities and bore our diseases" (Mt 8:17).
- He entrusted the ministry of healing to his disciples, telling them: "Cure the sick" (Mt 10:8).
- He instituted two sacraments in particular for the sick: the Eucharist (as Viaticum) and the Sacrament of the Anointing of the Sick.
- He taught those who followed him to transcend suffering and to give it a salvific meaning.
- He invited all his followers to be willing to suffer with him and like him: "Whoever wishes to come after me must deny himself, take up his cross, and follow me" (Mt 16:24).
- He pledged his help: "My grace is sufficient for you, for power is made perfect in weakness" (2 Cor 12:9).
- He continues to be with us and for us, above all in our moments of suffering.

✠ But Jesus Christ also did much more:

- He himself lived suffering, to the point of death, death on the Cross.
- He not only gave a *meaning* to suffering but also conferred a new *power* on it, a mysterious fecundity.
- He triumphed, in his Resurrection, over suffering and death, for himself and for us.

What does the Church do for the sick?

The Church, in its constant concern for the sick

- Proclaims and bears witness to the Gospel of suffering illuminated by the faith
- Has always accompanied and will continue to accompany the preaching of the Gospel, with initiatives of assistance and care on behalf of countless suffering people
- Offers its own specific contribution through the human and spiritual accompaniment of the sick
- Invites us to open ourselves to God's message of love, always attentive to the tears of those who turn to him
- Upholds the importance of pastoral care of the sick, in which hospital chapels play a special role, contributing so much to those who are hospitalized
- Fosters the development of the precious contribution that is made by volunteers, who with their service give rise to that vision of charity that infuses hope even into the human experience of suffering. It is also by means of these volunteers that Jesus can continue to walk among us today, to benefit and heal us.

What is the task of medicine?

The task of medicine is to

- Serve life always, promoting and defending it from conception to natural death. Even when it knows that it cannot eradicate a grave pathology, it dedicates its capacities to alleviating the suffering it causes.

- Recognize and respect, or at least not rule out, the transcendent moral and spiritual dimension of human life
- Realize and increase scientific research and progress
  - As a formidable instrument to improve conditions of life and well-being
  - In respect of the intangibility of every single human being
  - Avoiding any attempt at coercion and domination
- Reflect constantly and carefully on the very nature of human beings, on their dignity of having been created by God in his image and likeness. This inviolable dignity of human beings
  - Places them at the center and summit of all that exists on earth
  - Finds its foundation
    - In the mystery of creation, and in that of the redemption achieved by Jesus Christ, the eternal Son of God, Word of Life
    - In the destination of human beings, who are called to be children of God in the Son (Jesus Christ) and living temples of the Holy Spirit, in the perspective of eternal life in beatifying communion with God
  - Must be respected in whatever circumstances or conditions human beings may find themselves, and whatever stage of growth (embryo, fetus,

child, adult, elderly, dying). Not even suffering, lack of conscious awareness, or the imminence of death diminish the intrinsic dignity of the person.

- Recall that the service of medicine to life and to health is always and in every case a service that is tied to the meaning of suffering and death
- Allow itself to be enlivened by Christian inspiration, which does not take anything away from humanity and scientific research but rather supports it, illuminates it, and directs it toward the true and comprehensive well-being of every person and of the whole person
- Never forget that "the true measure of humanity is essentially determined in relationship to suffering and to the sufferer. This holds true both for the individual and for society. A society unable to accept its suffering members and incapable of helping to share their suffering and to bear it inwardly through 'com-passion' is a cruel and inhuman society" (*Spe Salvi*, no. 38).

What is the task of the physician?

The task of the physician is to

- Be a servant of life, which is always a good in itself and for itself, respecting it in whatever stage it may be, but above all in those in which it is weakest, like the initial and terminal phases

- Respect the ethical principles rooted in the Oath of Hippocrates itself, which states that
    - There are no lives unworthy of being lived
    - There are no sufferings, as distressing as they may be, that can justify the taking of a life
    - There are no reasons, as lofty as they may be, that make plausible the creation of human beings destined to be used and destroyed
- Make practical contributions to eliminating the causes of suffering that humiliate and sadden humanity, and to building a world ever more in keeping with the dignity of the human being
- Listen to every person, without any distinction or discrimination, and to welcome all in order to alleviate the sufferings of each one
- See in the sick person not a case number but a person to be approached with humanity and empathy. In spite of everything, the sick person remains greater than his or her illness, and his or her life greater than that which threatens it. To see medicine, therefore, as a service to the person, and not as power over the person.
- Treat the illness, but above all the sick person, keeping in mind the complementarity and interdependence of all the dimensions of the person (physical, affective, moral, spiritual, familial, social, etc.)
- Keep in mind that health is a reality that embraces the totality of the person, including all of his or her psychospiritual dynamism. Thus the healthy person is not simply the one in good physical or psychological

health but the one who is also in good spiritual health.

- Reach a proper balance between therapeutic insistence and desistence, avoiding therapeutic aggressiveness and experimentalism
- Meet the needs of the whole person, remembering that the only truly human response, in the face of another's suffering, is the love that pours itself out in companionship and sharing
- Add to the irreplaceable contribution of his or her professionalism the "heart," which is alone capable of reaching the "heart" of the sick person and humanizing structures
- Make his or her decisions while keeping three levels of assessment in mind: legal, ethical, and moral
- Live out his or her profession as a gift of self to the sick person (professional charity). "The specific mission that qualifies your medical and surgical profession consists in fulfilling three objectives:
    - "To cure the patient or at least endeavor to intervene effectively to prevent the development of the disease
    - "To alleviate the painful symptoms that accompany it, especially in the advanced stages
    - "And to attend to all the sick person's human expectations. . . .

"The aim must be a real therapeutic partnership with the patient, based on the specific clinical practice that permits the doctor to perceive the most appropriate means of communication suited to the individual patient. . . .

"The insistence with which today the patient's individual autonomy is emphasized must also be geared to promoting an approach to the sick person which, rightly, does not consider him an antagonist but rather an active and responsible collaborator in his treatment. . . . On the one hand, it is undeniable that the patient's self-determination should be respected, but without forgetting that the individualistic exaltation of autonomy ends by leading to a non-realistic and certainly impoverished interpretation of human reality. On the other, the physician's professional responsibility should lead him to suggest a treatment that strives for the true good of the patient, in the awareness that in his professional capacity he is usually able to evaluate the situation better than the patient himself.

"It is very important instead not to exclude from the therapeutic relationship the patient's normal environment and, in particular, his family. For this, it is essential to encourage in his relatives a sense of responsibility with regard to their family member" (Pope Benedict XVI, Address to participants in the national congress of the Italian Surgery Society, October 20, 2008).

- Remember that there is a directly proportional relationship between the capacity to suffer and the capacity to help those who suffer. The one who is willing to accept and bear his or her own sufferings with interior strength and serenity is also the person most sensitive to the pain of others and most dedicated to alleviating the pain of others.
- Practice true compassion, which
    - Promotes every reasonable effort to foster the healing of the patient
    - Accompanies the patient with love, respect, and dedication during the entire course of his or her illness, mobilizing all the action and all the attention possible to reduce suffering and to foster as serene an experience as possible
    - Listens to the requests of the sick person, who indeed has the right, for example, to ask for the suspension of a treatment. This does not mean, however, that the physician must agree to this request, especially when this would involve an act of euthanasia.
    - Stimulates solidarity and sharing not only with and for those who suffer without hope of recovery, but also with and for those experiencing the suffering of a loved one. At the same time, it makes it easier to accept when nothing can be done anymore to promote healing.

What is the task of the Catholic physician?

The mission of the Catholic physician is to

- Fulfill the tasks described above that are common to all physicians, with greater dedication and in a spirit of selflessness, bearing witness to Christ's love for the sick
- Pay attention to the spiritual dimension of the human person, with a keen awareness of the Christian meaning of life and death, and the role of suffering in human life
- Respect the law of God always and faithfully, even resorting to conscientious objection if human law contradicts divine law
- Be able to recognize in every sick person Christ himself, the features of his divine face. In taking care of the sick person, Christians know that they are taking care of Christ himself (see Mt 25:35-40).
- Draw upon the Christian faith for strength in one's own suffering and the capacity to alleviate the suffering of others
- Be an instrument of the merciful love of God
- Be the transparency of Christ, who, as the Good Samaritan par excellence, takes care of the sick
- Collaborate with those who work in pastoral care for the suffering
- Enliven his or her medical service with constant prayer to God, "lover of life" (Wis 11:26), always remembering that healing ultimately comes from the

Most High, through the special intercession of the Virgin Mary, invoked as *Salus infirmorum* and *Mater Scientiae*

- Mobilize not only medical treatment, but also spiritual care, which constitutes not only a felt need but even a fundamental right of every sick person, with the consequent responsibility of those who attend to them
- Examine his or her own spirituality, the system of values that guides his or her existence, the answers that arise within the heart to the questions concerning the meaning of suffering and death
- Bring Christian comfort to the sick and to their family members
- Encourage the sick to ask for and receive in faith the sacraments that Christ has instituted partly in order to provide spiritual help to the sick person: the Sacraments of Confession, the Eucharist (in particular as Viaticum) and the Anointing of the Sick

What are the positive aspects that come from illness?

Illness can

- Help us to realize our limitations, our human fragility, the temporary nature of our journey here on earth
- Give rise to a broad, close-knit network of solidarity on the family and social (volunteer) level. Only a purely utilitarian conception leads to the belief that

a person's illness is always and in every case a deficit on the personal, familial, and social level.

- Offer the possibility of knowing how to interpret God's plan for one's life. The "key" of this interpretation is the Cross of Christ. The Incarnate Word came to meet our weakness by taking it on himself in the mystery of the Cross. Those who are able to welcome it in their lives experience how pain, illuminated by faith, can become a source of hope and salvation.
- Constitute a concrete possibility, offered to our freedom, to decide what should be the fulfillment of our existence
- Give everyone the opportunity to suffer with the other, uniting the suffering of both with that of Christ, and offering it on behalf of others.

    It can also have redemptive value for ourselves and for others. If our suffering is united with that of Christ, it participates in the salvific work of Jesus Christ. It becomes a means and a living sacrifice for the salvation of the world and can bring moral and spiritual benefits to the patient and to humanity. "In my flesh I am filling up what is lacking in the afflictions of Christ on behalf of his body, which is the church" (Col 1:24).
- Invite us to make the words of Job our own: "We accept good things from God; should we not accept evil? . . . The Lord gave and the Lord has taken away; blessed be the name of the Lord!" (Job 2:10, 1:21).

It helps us to discover the true face of God: the reality of evil, of suffering, of war, does not induce us to deny God, but rather "helps to purify all false concepts of God and leads us to discover his true face: the face of a God who, in Christ, has taken upon himself the wounds of injured humanity . . . The Lord has not taken away suffering and evil from the world but has vanquished them at their roots by the superabundance of his grace" (Pope Benedict XVI, Message "Urbi et Orbi," Easter 2007).

What benefits does the Sacrament of the Anointing of the Sick bring?

This sacrament, instituted by Christ not for the dead, but for the living, and therefore for the Christian who is seriously ill

- Confers a special gift of the Holy Spirit: a grace of comfort, peace, and courage to
  - Face the difficulties of the illness
  - Unite ourselves more intimately with the Passion of Christ
  - Contribute to the good of the People of God
- Forgives all sins, if it has not been possible to celebrate the Sacrament of Confession first
- Sometimes promotes healing, if this is good for the spiritual salvation of the sick person
- Prepares the person for the transition into eternal life
- Allows the person to benefit from the prayer of the whole Church, which

- Intercedes on behalf of the sick person
- Suffers together with him or her
- Offers itself, through Christ, to God the Father

What is to be done for the terminally ill?

✠ It should be kept in mind that the Lord of life is present with the sick person as the One who lives and gives life, the One who said, "I came so that they might have life and have it more abundantly" (Jn 10:10), "I am the resurrection and the life; whoever believes in me, even if he dies, will live" (Jn 11:25), and "I will raise him on the last day" (Jn 6:54).

✠ Within this life that is being extinguished should be seen a new birth and a renewed existence, offered by the Risen One to those who have not deliberately opposed his love. Death is the conclusion of earthly experience, but death also opens for each one of us, beyond time, the full and definitive life.

Every person should be guaranteed the necessary support through adequate medical therapies and interventions, identified and managed according to the criteria of medical proportionality, always taking into account the moral necessity of administering (on the part of the physician) and accepting (on the part of the patient) those means of preserving life which, in a particular situation, can be considered "ordinary." But as for treatments that are significantly risky or can be prudently judged "extraordinary," recourse to these will be considered morally licit, but optional.

The person who is incurably ill should be prepared for death, being told the truth gently, choosing the suitable time and language, avoiding any well-meaning but misguided silence, and above all proclaiming where the "life that does not die" is possible.

Every person should be guaranteed the necessary medical care, and above all psychological and emotional support. "Even when a cure can no longer be hoped for much can be done for the patient. His suffering can be alleviated, and above all, it is possible to accompany him on his way, improving the quality of his life as much as possible. This is not something to be underestimated, because every individual patient, even one who is incurable, bears an inherent unconditional value, a dignity to be honored, that constitutes the indispensable basis of every medical intervention" (Address to participants in the national congress of the Italian Surgery Society).

Support should be guaranteed for families that intend to provide care in the home, sometimes for long periods of time, for loved ones afflicted with degenerative pathologies (cancer, neurological disorders, etc.) or in need of particularly demanding assistance.

Labor laws should also extend to relatives under the stress of caring for a terminally ill person the same rights that are usually granted to parents when a child is born.

Any form of direct euthanasia must be avoided (see Pope Benedict XVI, Address to the Pontifical Academy for Life, February 25, 2008).

What is the Christian conception of palliative care?

✠ The Christian faith recognizes the need for palliative care in some cases that "seek to make suffering more bearable in the final stages of illness and to ensure that the patient is supported and accompanied in his or her ordeal" (Pope John Paul II, *Evangelium Vitae*, no. 65). In fact, they seek to alleviate, especially in the terminal patient, a vast spectrum of symptoms of physical, psychological, and mental suffering, and therefore require the intervention of a team of specialists with adequate medical, psychological, and religious training, working together to support the patient in the critical phase.

At the same time, it affirms the need to respect the freedom of the patient, who must be allowed, as far as possible, "to satisfy their moral and family duties, and above all they ought to be able to prepare in a fully conscious way for their definitive meeting with God" (op. cit., no. 65).

✠ The Christian faith recommends that the administration of analgesics be proportional to the intensity of the pain and its treatment, avoiding any form of euthanasia, such as administering enormous amounts of analgesics with the intention of causing death.

✠ The Christian faith recalls the principle of double effect as related to the use of such drugs. On the one hand, these certainly alleviate pain, but on the other they can cause dependence or even accelerate the lethal effect of the illness.

✠ The Christian faith encourages the training of specialists in palliative care, in particular with the creation of educational institutions that could also be of interest to psychologists or pastoral workers, as well as hospice homes for the terminally ill, remembering that as early as the first century, at the time of Pope St. Cletus—the third successor of St. Peter—the Church had provided for their construction.

What does the Christian faith say about aggressive medical treatment?

✠ The Christian faith affirms that

- Rejecting aggressive treatment does not mean the patient is rejecting his or her life
- The object of deliberation over the appropriateness of beginning or continuing a course of treatment is not the value of the patient's life but the value of the medical treatment for the patient
- The decision not to begin or to stop a treatment is to be held as ethically correct when this would be ineffective or clearly disproportional to the purposes of keeping alive or curing the patient
- The rejection of aggressive treatment is therefore an expression of the respect that is due to the patient at all times
- It is not aggressive treatment to ensure the sick person, if available, artificial respiration, nutrition and hydration, and treatment for pain

Saying yes to life therefore also requires the rejection of both aggressive treatment and euthanasia. And this applies to both dimensions:

- It applies to aggressive treatment, which says: I have the power to keep death away.

- It applies to euthanasia, which says: I have the power to anticipate death.

Neither of these uses correct logic, because both take the perspective of "I own life and I am the one who decides when it begins, how long it lasts, when it ends . . ."

✠ Thus every person of good will should say

- Three "yeses":
    - To life
    - To palliative care
    - To adequate assistance for the sick and for the elderly
- Threes "nos":
    - To euthanasia
    - To aggressive treatment
    - To the abandonment of the most fragile

Are artificial nutrition and hydration considered aggressive treatment?

No.

✠ "The administration of food and water even by artificial means is, in principle, an ordinary and proportionate means of preserving life. It is therefore obligatory to the extent to which, and for as long as, it is shown to accomplish its proper finality, which is the hydration and nourishment of the patient. In this way suffering and death by starvation and dehydration are prevented" (CDF, *Responses to Certain Questions of the United States Conference of Catholic Bishops Concerning Artificial Nutrition and Hydration*). Even when competent physicians judge with moral certainty that the patient will never regain consciousness, "a patient in a 'permanent vegetative state' is a person with fundamental human dignity and must, therefore, receive ordinary and proportionate care which includes, in principle, the administration of water and food even by artificial means" (op. cit.).

✠ It must also not be forgotten that

- No expert can, at the present time, declare the irreversibility of a vegetative state, except on the basis of a purely subjective decision
- The declaration of a moment clearly cannot be taken as a person's will regarding decisions like those that concern opposition or lack thereof to a treatment that, among other things, is on the edge between treatment and nutrition

When will sickness, suffering, and death come to an end?

They will end when Christ the Lord returns at the end of time, to free the universe from corruption and death, and to renew it with "new heavens and a new earth" (2 Pt 3:13).

✠

For more on this topic, see the following pontifical documents:

Catechism of the Catholic Church, nos. 309-314; 1499-1525

Compendium of the CCC, nos. 57-58; 313-320

Pope John Paul II, *Salvifici Doloris*, 1984; *Evangelium Vitae*, 1995

Congregation for the Doctrine of the Faith, *Donum Vitae*, 1987; *Responses to Certain Questions of the United States Conference of Catholic Bishops Concerning Artificial Nutrition and Hydration*, August 1, 2007

IX
Money

How should money and wealth be considered?

✠ Money is neither good nor evil, from a moral point of view. In itself, money is a material reality that—in that it is created by God—is good. It is a means of exchange, the value of which is established by convention in a society.

✠ It is in reference to the person that money can become good or evil. This depends on

- How the person acquires it: honestly, or by theft or deceit
- How the person relates to it. It has value, and it has great influence in human life, but it is not and must not become the main, sole, or highest value of human beings, who must do all they can to avoid becoming enslaved to it.
- How it is used

When is the use of money moral?

When the person uses it

- With the awareness of being an administrator and beneficiary, giving it its proper importance and value: material goods are means, they are not the end of human life
- For one's own good, for that of one's family, for the good of one's neighbor
- Keeping in mind various criteria, for example, obligatory expenses for necessities; discretional expenditures; the need to save in view of future necessities (while still trusting in providence); the needs of others, above all those who lack even what is necessary and indispensable in order to live
- While respecting its "universal destination," in the sense that the goods of this world must be used so that no one goes without that which is necessary

When is the use of money immoral?

All of these are immoral:

- Any undue accumulation of material goods
- Any attachment to them: "The love of money is the root of all evils" (1 Tm 6:10). "Where your treasure is, there also will your heart be" (Mt 6:21).
- The theory that makes profit the exclusive rule and ultimate end of economic activity

- Any practice that reduces persons to being nothing other than pure instruments of profit: everything that subjugates human beings, leads to the idolatry of money, and contributes to the spread of atheism. "You cannot serve God and mammon" (Mt 6:24); "It is easier for a camel to pass through [the] eye of [a] needle than for one who is rich to enter the kingdom of God" (Mk 10:25).

What harm can money do?

It can cause serious harm.

✠ Within the person himself or herself, money can become

- A way to enslave the person, and this takes place when it becomes the end and master, instead of being a means and servant
- An instrument of the will to power that can blind reason
- A way to give preference to having, before and more than the being of the person
- A decisive or even exclusive criterion for determining the value of oneself and of the other: an individual is worth as much as he or she possesses
- A *condicio sine qua non* for the realization of the person as a person
- A cause of constant dissatisfaction and unhappiness, above all when the logic of accumulation prevails in the person

- A great cause of coercion. True freedom is lost when one becomes obsessed with acquiring money, possessing it, protecting it, defending it, administering it . . . to the point of becoming its slave. But if one acquires and uses it honestly, money can be a source of freedom: it brings rapidity and efficiency, permitting access to the best things for oneself and for others.

✠ In one's relationship with God, money can

- Become an absolute, which replaces the true God; one lives a genuine worship of money
- Lead to the rejection of God, or to living as if God did not exist

✠ In one's relationship with others, money can

- Increase the distance between rich and poor
- Encourage the commission of injustice, theft, and fraud
- Become a *status symbol*, which brings recognition and advantages in society
- Lead to the rejection of others. The great disgrace of turning money into an idol is the fact that it separates one from others. The richer one becomes, the more one risks not seeing and not listening to others. The goods of this world, which should be a sign of communication, of communion, thus become an obstacle, a wall between us and others, a wall made of prestige, of different customs, of greater possibilities.

- Be a cause of divisions (even within the family itself) and of numerous conflicts that disturb the social order, national and international

What is prohibited by the Tenth Commandment: You shall not covet your neighbor's belongings?

✠ "The tenth commandment forbids greed and the desire to amass earthly goods without limit. It forbids avarice arising from a passion for riches and their attendant power. It also forbids the desire to commit injustice by harming our neighbor in his temporal goods:

> When the Law says, "You shall not covet," these words mean that we should banish our desires for whatever does not belong to us. Our thirst for another's goods is immense, infinite, never quenched. Thus it is written: "He who loves money never has money enough."
>
> It is not a violation of this commandment to desire to obtain things that belong to one's neighbor, provided this is done by just means. Traditional catechesis realistically mentions "those who have a harder struggle against their criminal desires" and so who "must be urged the more to keep this commandment":
>
>> . . . merchants who desire scarcity and rising prices, who cannot bear not to be the only ones buying and selling so that they themselves can sell more dearly and buy more cheaply; those who hope that their peers will be impoverished, in order to realize a profit either by selling to them or buying from them . . .

physicians who wish disease to spread; lawyers who are eager for many important cases and trials. (CCC, nos. 2536-2537)

How must the Christian behave with regard to money?

In addition to observing everything already said here about the honest acquisition, moral use, and correct attitude toward money, the Christian must

- Combat greed, since this is the root of all evil. Ambrose Autpert writes, "From the soil of the earth different sharp thorns emerge from various roots, but in the human heart, the barbs of all the vices come from a single root: greed" (*De Cupiditate* 1: cccm 27b, p. 963).
- Be aware that giving money without giving oneself is a lie. Sharing means giving one's time, one's power, one's competencies, and the gifts received, to the extent of one's abilities.
- Keep in mind what Jesus said in the Gospel about the two small coins that the widow gave at the temple: "I tell you truly, this poor widow put in more than all the rest; for those others have all made offerings from their surplus wealth, but she, from her poverty, has offered her whole livelihood" (Lk 21:3-4).
- Practice a preferential love for the poor

Why and how should we love the poor?

The *Catechism of the Catholic Church* answers this question as follows (nos. 2443-2449):

✠ God blesses those who come to the aid of the poor and rebukes those who turn away from them: "Give to him who begs from you, do not refuse him who would borrow from you"; "you received without pay, give without pay." It is by what they have done for the poor that Jesus Christ will recognize his chosen ones.

✠ This love

- Is inspired by the Gospel of the Beatitudes, of the poverty of Jesus, and of his concern for the poor
- Is even one of the motives for the duty of working so as to 'be able to give to those in need'
- Extends not only to material poverty but also to the many forms of cultural and religious poverty
- Is incompatible with immoderate love of riches or their selfish use:

> Come now, you rich, weep and howl for the miseries that are coming upon you. Your riches have rotted and your garments are moth-eaten. Your gold and silver have rusted, and their rust will be evidence against you and will eat your flesh like fire. You have laid up treasure for the last days.

The works of mercy are charitable actions by which we come to the aid of our neighbor in his spiritual and bodily necessities. Instructing, advising, consoling, comforting are spiritual works of mercy, as are forgiving and bearing wrongs patiently. The corporal works of mercy consist especially in feeding the hungry, sheltering the homeless, clothing the naked, visiting the sick and imprisoned, and burying the dead. Among all these, giving alms to the poor is one of the chief witnesses to fraternal charity: it is also a work of justice pleasing to God:

> He who has two coats, let him share with him who has none and he who has food must do likewise. But give for alms those things which are within; and behold, everything is clean for you. If a brother or sister is ill-clad and in lack of daily food, and one of you says to them, "Go in peace, be warmed and filled," without giving them the things needed for the body, what does it profit?
>
> When her mother reproached her for caring for the poor and the sick at home, St. Rose of Lima said to her: "When we serve the poor and the sick, we serve Jesus. We must not fail to help our neighbors, because in them we serve Jesus."

What is Jesus Christ asking when he says: "Blessed are the poor in spirit" (Mt 5:3)?

✠ "Jesus enjoins his disciples to prefer him to everything and everyone, and bids them 'renounce all that [they have]' for his sake and that of the Gospel. Shortly before his passion he gave them the example of the poor widow of Jerusalem who, out of her poverty, gave all that she had to live on. The precept of detachment from riches is obligatory for entrance into the Kingdom of heaven.

✠ "All Christ's faithful are to 'direct their affections rightly, lest they be hindered in their pursuit of perfect charity by the use of worldly things and by an adherence to riches which is contrary to the spirit of evangelical poverty.'

✠ "The Beatitudes reveal an order of happiness and grace, of beauty and peace. Jesus celebrates the joy of the poor, to whom the Kingdom already belongs.

> The Word speaks of voluntary humility as 'poverty in spirit'; the Apostle gives an example of God's poverty when he says: 'For your sakes he became poor.'

✠ "The Lord grieves over the rich, because they find their consolation in the abundance of goods. 'Let the proud seek and love earthly kingdoms, but blessed are the poor in spirit for theirs is the Kingdom of heaven.' Abandonment to the providence of the Father in heaven frees us from anxiety about tomorrow. Trust in God is a preparation for the blessedness of the poor. They shall see God" (CCC, nos. 2544-2547).

What is the relationship between morality and the economy?

✠ There is a necessary distinction between the two: the economy has its own laws of production, distribution, and consumption of material goods and services.

✠ At the same time, the economy is not exempt from morality, in that the economy has its reason for being in the human person, it is at the service of the whole person and of all persons. Realized according to its own methods, economic activity must be exercised in the context of the moral order, with respect for social justice, in a way that corresponds with God's plan for humanity.

✠ The Church provides its moral judgment on economic and social matters when this is required by the fundamental rights of the person or by the salvation of souls. It seeks to inculcate the proper dispositions in the relationship with earthly goods and in socio-economic relationships.

What are the tasks of the economy according to Christian ethics?

These are multiple and complementary:

✠ With regard to the person, the economy must

- Promote the dignity of the human person and the good of all humanity
- Protect the liberty of the person in the economic sector as a fundamental value and inalienable right. The true capital to be valued, protected, and invested in is the human person.
- Foster the harmonization of the professional creative capacity—both of the individual and of the business—with moral principles

✠ With regard to society, the economy must

- Achieve its growth, but not at the expense of human beings, of entire peoples and social groups, condemned to indigence and exclusion
- Foster the equal availability and distribution of goods and services in transparency and legality, including the development of more equal and fair trade
- Practice solidarity within families and society, and among nations
- Have as its subjects all persons and all peoples, in that all are responsible for all
- Seek an increase of wealth that is not only quantitative, but qualitative, directing this progress to the comprehensive and supportive development of the human person and society. The legitimate effort to make a fair profit, the criteria of economic efficiency, must be harmonized with the protection of the dignity of the person. One has the duty to consider the good of persons, and not only the increase of profits. These, however, are necessary: they permit investments capable of ensuring the future of companies and guaranteeing employment.
- Seek to eliminate inequalities and imbalances that cause situations of extreme poverty. On the international level, the inequality of economic means and resources is such that it produces a true "chasm" among nations. On the one side are those who possess and increase the means of development, and on the other, those who accumulate debts (see Pope

John Paul II, encyclical letter *Sollicitudo Rei Socialis*, no. 14).

- Foster a reasonable regulation of the market and of economic initiatives, according to a just hierarchy of values in view of the common good. Allowing the market to regulate itself cannot achieve social justice, because there are many human needs that do not have access to the market.

What is at the basis of all authentic economic growth?

✠ At the basis of all authentic and complete development of human society is the growth of the sense of God and of self-knowledge.

✠ In this case, development

- Multiplies material goods and puts them at the service of the person and of his or her freedom
- Reduces economic misery and exploitation
- Increases respect for cultural identities and openness to transcendence

What is the role of the state in terms of the economy, according to the Christian conception?

The responsibility of the state is great, and at the same time limited and specific. "Economic activity, especially the activity of a market economy, cannot be conducted in an institutional, juridical or political vacuum. On the contrary, it presupposes sure guarantees of individual freedom and private property, as well as a stable currency and efficient public services. Hence the principle task of the state is to guarantee this security, so that those who work and produce can enjoy the fruits of their labors and thus feel encouraged to work efficiently and honestly . . . Another task of the state is that of overseeing and directing the exercise of human rights in the economic sector. However, primary responsibility in this area belongs not to the State but to individuals and to the various groups and associations which make up society" (Pope John Paul II, encyclical letter *Centesimus Annus*, no. 48).

How can people help each other?

✠ "*Rich nations* have a grave moral responsibility toward those which are unable to ensure the means of their development by themselves or have been prevented from doing so by tragic historical events. It is a duty in solidarity and charity; it is also an obligation in justice if the prosperity of the rich nations has come from resources that have not been paid for fairly.

✠ "*Direct aid* is an appropriate response to immediate, extraordinary needs caused by natural catastrophes, epidemics, and the like. But it does not suffice to repair the grave damage resulting from destitution or to provide a lasting solution to a country's needs. It is also necessary to *reform* international economic and financial *institutions* so that they will better promote equitable relationships with less advanced countries. The efforts of poor countries working for growth and liberation must be supported. This doctrine must be applied especially in the area of agricultural labor. Peasants, especially in the Third World, form the overwhelming majority of the poor" (CCC, nos. 2439-2440).

✠

For more on this topic, see the following pontifical documents:

Catechism of the Catholic Church, Part Three
Compendium of the CCC, Part Three
Pope John Paul II, *Sollicitudo Rei Socialis*; *Centesimus Annus*
Pontifical Council for Justice and Peace, *Compendium of the Social Doctrine of the Church*

X
Work

What are the positive aspects of work?

Work has multiple and complementary dimensions:

✠ The human dimension: Work is one of the highest forms of

- Human growth
- The expression and affirmation of oneself and one's abilities
- The exercise of social responsibilities
- Personal and communal retraining and updating
- Openness to and solidarity with the world

✠ The family dimension: It constitutes an essential means that makes possible the foundation of a family, whose means of support comes precisely through work.

✠ The social dimension: It improves society, fostering better economic and social conditions, above all on behalf of the neediest.

✠ The cosmic dimension: It is a source of the enrichment and transformation of creation. Through work, the human person governs the world together with God, is lord over it together with him, and does good things for self and others, appreciating natural resources.

What is the relationship between the human person and work?

By working, human beings

- Perfect themselves in their humanity
- Express the free and fecund gift of self
- Exercise their physical, intellectual, and spiritual faculties
    - By creating works of art and of thought
    - By discovering new things
    - By producing goods and services
- Make themselves useful to others
- Draw the means of support for their lives, for those of their relatives, and for the human community
- Have the right to a just wage
- Transform nature, while respecting it

In what way is work for the person?

✠ Work is a right, and not a privilege. Access to work must be open to all, without unjust discrimination. Every person has the right to honest and secure work, although this is not the only and not even the main reason of life. Work must be considered a good for all, which must be available to all who are capable of it. "Full employment" must be a goal for any economic system directed to justice and to the common good.

✠ Work is also a duty for every person: "If anyone [is] unwilling to work, neither should that one eat" (2 Thes 3:10).

✠ All work, if it is honest, is worthy of respect.

✠ The person is the subject and the recipient of work. Work is an *actus personae*, it is for the human person; the human person is not for work. The person is the measure of the dignity of work. Work proceeds from the person and is also essentially directed and finalized to it.

✠ In work, the person

- Considers the other as "another self," and not as a competitor or a slave. Work is and must be with and for others, and not against others.
- Uses the fruits of work also as an opportunity for exchange, for relations and encounter
- Appreciates, collaborates with, and respects the talent and experience that only the older ones can bring to work

✠ One must therefore recognize the dignity of human work as a duty and perfecting of human beings, a beneficial exercise of their custody of creation, a service of the community, a prolongation of the work of the Creator, a contribution to the plan of salvation (see *Gaudium et Spes*, no. 34).

What are the conditions for good work?

✠ Here are the main conditions for good work:

- Respect and promotion of the dignity of the person and the inalienable rights of the worker
- The freedom to create and participate in public associations to promote and defend one's own values and rights
- Access to and participation in economic progress, in the management and use of one's work
- The making of contributions (established by the legitimate authority) to the institutions of social security
- Fair compensation, which
  - Also takes into account the age and the personal abilities of the worker as well as the needs of any family members, especially children
  - Seeks a just balance between merit and need
- Full occupation
- Limited work hours; humane work schedules
- Better coordination of work time and the time dedicated to human and family relations
- Legitimate rest
- Promotion of the health and safety of workers
- Ongoing human and technical education
- Respect for the hierarchy of values, which puts the person who works in first place
- Suitable conditions of health and hygiene in the workplace
- Respect for the environment

✠ Everyone, according to his or her opportunities and abilities, must work to create or increase, for self and for others, these positive conditions that foster good work.

What are the negative aspects of work to be avoided or eliminated?

✠ Here are the main aspects:

- Suppression of the dignity of the person
- The exploitation of self, others, and nature
- Unemployment, which offends the dignity of the person and threatens the balance of life and the possibility of founding and raising a family
- Unjustified recourse to second jobs or overtime, above all when this is done to obtain the "superfluous." This takes jobs away from others and also takes away time and energy that could be dedicated to the development of personal dimensions (above all religious-spiritual), to one's family, or to volunteer initiatives.
- Absenteeism, lack of effort
- The indiscriminate increase of work over Sundays and holidays
- Destruction of the environment
- Wasting time and resources, capital flight, fraud
- Abusive—if not outright usurious—financial systems, unfair trade relations
- Excessive accumulation and concentration of the means of production, distribution, and consumption

- Dishonest use of the means of communication
- Unjustified dismissal
- Work of uncertain duration, especially for young people: "When lack of steady work does not permit young people to have a family of their own, society's authentic and full development is seriously jeopardized" (Pope Benedict XVI, Letter to the president of the Italian bishops' conference on the occasion of the centenary of the Catholic Social Week, October 18, 2007).
- Class warfare
- Indiscriminate strikes

✠ It must also be recognized that, in spite of the commitment of each one and of all, it will never be possible to eliminate all these negative aspects completely. The Christian knows that their total and definitive elimination will take place when, at the end of this world, God will make "new heavens and a new earth" (2 Pt 3:13).

What is meant by the common good, to which work is also directed?

✠ What is meant is the entirety of those conditions of social life that allow groups, as well as their individual members, to reach their perfection as completely and quickly as possible. It involves three essential elements:

- Respect for the person, for his or her fundamental and inalienable rights, such as the possibility of acting according to the upright dictates of conscience,

- the protection of private life, and proper freedom in the area of religion as well
- The social well-being and the development of the spiritual and material goods of the individual, of families, and of society
- Peace, meaning the stability and security of a just order

✠ At the same time, it must be kept in mind that the economic prosperity of a people is not measured exclusively by the quantity of goods produced, but also taking into account

- The way in which they are produced
- The level of equality in the distribution of the profits from them
- The attainment of the comprehensive development of every person

How does the Christian behave at work?

When working, in addition to realizing and completing the aforementioned positive aspects valid for every person, the Christian

- Actualizes his or her identity as a human being created in the image of God. Work belongs to the original condition of human beings, established by God as the custodians of creation, and precedes Original Sin. It is thus neither a punishment nor a curse.
- Cooperates with the providential plan of God, Creator and Redeemer: God calls human beings to

"cultivate and care for" (Gn 2:15) the gifts he has created. Human beings are not masters, but administrators, tenants, caretakers, called upon to reflect, in their work, the imprint of the One in whose image they are.

- Imitates Jesus Christ, the carpenter of Nazareth, who dedicated the majority of his life on earth to manual labor
- Cooperates with him in his work of redemption. By following the teachings on work of Christ and of the Church, and working with commitment and suffering, the Christian shows himself or herself as a disciple of Christ, bearing the cross every day.
- Recognizes that work, in its fatigue and suffering, is a sign and fruit of Original Sin. Since then, the soil has become stingy, ungrateful, blindly hostile (see Gn 4:12), it requires the sweat of the human brow (see Gn 3:17, 19).
- Strives along with others to eliminate or at least diminish the negative aspects of work
- Participates in the divine art and wisdom and beautifies creation, the cosmos already ordered by God the Father
- Helps the weakest and neediest
- Sanctifies himself or herself and others
- Recognizes that work is essential, but that God, and not work, is the source of life and the end of the human person
- Gives glory to God

- Finds an opportunity for contemplation and prayer: *ora et labora* ("pray and work")
- Serves the family and social community according to the plan of God
- Builds up the Kingdom of God

What is the relationship between human work and the integrity of creation?

"The seventh commandment enjoins respect for the integrity of creation. Animals, like plants and inanimate beings, are by nature destined for the common good of past, present, and future humanity. Use of the mineral, vegetable, and animal resources of the universe cannot be divorced from respect for moral imperatives. Man's dominion over inanimate and other living beings granted by the Creator is not absolute; it is limited by concern for the quality of life of his neighbor, including generations to come; it requires a religious respect for the integrity of creation" (CCC, no. 2415).

What is required by solidarity in work?

Solidarity requires

- The commitment of each one to cooperate with the others in creating and improving the conditions of work and society
- The fair distribution of the goods and fruits of work
- The commitment to a more just social order, in which tensions and conflicts are resolved with negotiation and dialogue

- Collaboration among all: rich and poor, owners and employees, nations and peoples, rejecting hatred and class warfare
- The possibility of free associations (e.g., labor unions, business owners' groups . . .), avoiding corporate dominance
- The commitment on behalf of the poorest
- The development of the positive aspects of globalization for the purpose of achieving a humanization of work on the planetary level
- The virtue of solidarity, which actualizes the sharing of spiritual gifts even more than material ones

What virtues are realized in work?

In work, "respect for human dignity requires the practice of the virtue of *temperance*, so as to moderate attachment to this world's goods; the practice of the virtue of *justice*, to preserve our neighbor's rights and render him what is his due; and the practice of *solidarity*, in accordance with the golden rule and in keeping with the generosity of the Lord, who 'though he was rich, yet for your sake . . . became poor so that by his poverty, you might become rich'" (CCC, no. 2407).

What kinds of primacy must be respected in the field of work?

Respect must be given to the primacy of

- The human person over work and over things
- Spirit over matter

- Ethics over technology. Not all that is technologically feasible is also morally acceptable.
- Labor over capital, which remains only an instrument or the instrumental cause of work. At the same time, there is a certain complementarity between labor and capital: capital cannot do without labor, nor labor without capital.
- The universal destination of goods over the nonetheless legitimate freedom of both economic initiative and private property

What is the basis of the universal destination of goods, and what does it entail?

The universal destination of goods

- Is based on the fact that God, in creating, has given the earth, with all its goods, to the whole human race
- Entails
  - The fair distribution of goods within every country and among countries
  - The co-responsibility of all for creation and for past, present, and future generations
  - The fact that the authority of the state should be placed at the service of each and of all

What are the characteristics of the individual right to private property?

✠ There is a right to private property, acquired or received in a just manner. This is expressed in the possession of material goods, of means of production, of consumer goods, of free access to the knowledge and application of science and technology.

✠ This right has these characteristics:

- It is valid for all.
- It must be guaranteed and regulated with adequate civil laws, in which any abuses must be avoided (e.g., plantation economy).
- It is at the service of the comprehensive growth of the person.

The right to private property must be implemented in a just way, practicing the virtues of

- Temperance, in order to moderate attachment to the goods of this world
- Justice, in order to respect the rights of one's neighbor and give him or her what is due
- Solidarity, in order to share generously with those who have less than we do

✠ This right is not absolute. It must be tempered with concern for the needs of others, the quality of life of one's neighbor, and respect for the integrity of creation.

✠ It is subordinated to the right of the common use and universal destination of goods. "In using them, therefore, a man should regard his lawful possessions not merely as his own but also as common property in the sense that they should accrue to the benefit of not only himself but of others" (*Gaudium et Spes*, no. 69).

What are the positive aspects of the right to private property?

Private property has its natural lawfulness in that it can have the following positive aspects:

- It can provide the space necessary for personal and familial autonomy.
- It can be an expression and prolongation of human freedom.
- It can contribute to personal security.
- It is the legitimate fruit of personal savings.
- It can provide an opportunity to make a personal contribution to society and to the economy.
- It can be an incentive for greater initiative.
- It can be a means for creating new jobs.

What are the criteria of a just wage?

"Payment for labor must be such as to furnish a man with the means to cultivate his own material, social, cultural, and spiritual life worthily, and that of his dependents. What this payment should be will vary according to each man's assignment and productivity, the conditions of his place of employment, and the common good" (*Gaudium et Spes*, no. 67).

When is it legitimate to resort to striking?

Here are some conditions for the legitimacy of recourse to striking:

- It is an extreme or extraordinary means, or at least necessary for the sake of proportional advantage.
- It is to be undertaken after all other means of overcoming conflicts have been ineffective.
- It must be done through peaceful means, avoiding any sort of violence.
- It must respect the freedom of others, rejecting pickets and boycotts.
- It must respect the fundamental rights of the community (above all of the weakest and most defenseless).
- It must guarantee the fundamental services of society.
- It must pursue objectives related to the conditions of work and respectful of the common good.

✠

For more on this topic, see the following pontifical documents:

Pope Leo XIII, *Rerum Novarum*, 1982
Pope John Paul II, *Laborem Exercens*, 1981
Catechism of the Catholic Church, nos. 531-533; 2184-2188; 2427-2435
Compendium of the CCC, nos. 503-520
Pontifical Council for Justice and Peace, *Compendium of the Social Doctrine of the Church*, pp. 144-177.

XI
Politics

What have relations between Christians and politics been like over the centuries?

✠ Down through the centuries and in different countries, relations between politics and Christians, between state and Church, have gone through a complex evolution both on the level of principle and on the level of practical application.

✠ The manner of conceiving and realizing these relations takes into account the different historical, social, and ecclesial contexts.

✠ My reflection, explained below, is based in particular on the ecclesial documents of the last fifty years, and above all on *Gaudium et Spes* of Vatican Council II, the *Catechism of the Catholic Church*, the *Code of Canon Law*, and the *Compendium of the Social Doctrine of the Church* (SDC).

What is the aim of politics according to the Christian faith?

Politics, understood as multifaceted and varied economic, social, legislative, administrative, cultural activity, must

✠ With regard to the person and to civil society:

- Protect and promote the fundamental and inalienable rights of the person, the dignity and equality of all citizens
- Perform its tasks as a service to persons and to society
- Promote fundamental values and use just and suitable means to realize the common good, justice, and peace
- Use the natural virtues described so well by the ancient Greeks, which are the four cardinal virtues: prudence, justice, fortitude, and temperance

✠ With regard to public authority:

- Use honest means to obtain, maintain, and increase this authority
- Exercise with impartiality and democracy the mandate received from the citizens
- Foster the education and democratic participation of citizens, respecting the principle of solidarity, above all toward the poorest
- Establish transparency in personal and public administration, with the honest use of public money
- Protect the right to political opposition

✠ With regard to humanity:

- Promote the solidarity, prosperity, and peace of all peoples
- Resolve any conflicts with dialogue
- Establish and reinforce an international order, with respect for those principles that inspire a legal order in harmony with the moral order
- Realize the common good

What are the requirements of the common good?

✠ The common good

- Is made concrete in "the sum of those conditions of social life which allow social groups and their individual members relatively thorough and ready access to their own fulfillment" (*Gaudium et Spes*, no. 26)
- "Belonging to everyone and to each person . . . is and remains 'common,' because it is indivisible and because only together is it possible to attain it, increase it and safeguard its effectiveness, with regard also to the future" (*Compendium of the SDC*, no. 164)

✠ The common good

- Is "the good of *everyone* and the good of each person taken as a *whole*" (*Christifideles Laici*, no. 42)
- Demands that "there must be made available to all men everything necessary for leading a life truly human" (*Gaudium et Spes*, no. 26)

- Has to do with a comprehensive conception of human beings and their development, according to all the richness of its articulations
- Entails the commitment of all and of each one, although with various and complementary forms, tasks, and responsibilities. It seeks "the good of all and of each individual, because we are all really responsible for all" (*Sollecitudo Rei Socialis*, no. 38). The common good of persons cannot be realized apart from the common good of the communities to which the persons belong.
- Also includes the economic dimension, although it is not exhausted by it. The common good involves the orderly interweaving of three indispensable strands of development: economic, social, and human.

When is a society authentically democratic, according to the Christian conception?

✠ When the society is founded on a legitimately constituted state, where the law is sovereign, and not the arbitrary will of human beings. Such a state requires

- Free and universal elections
- A correct conception of the dignity of human beings and the defense of their rights
- A consistent vision and implementation of the common good as the end and normative criterion of political life

- Widespread participation and shared responsibility at various levels and according to the respective capacities of all citizens
- Respect for the political, cultural, economic, and religious autonomy of oneself and of others

✠ In a democratic society, the subject of political authority is the people, considered in its totality as the bearer of sovereignty. The political community is constituted to be at the service of civil society, and therefore ultimately of the persons and groups that compose it. The political authority must therefore

- Guarantee the orderly and authentic life of the community, promoting the common good
- Respect the principle of subsidiarity, which means that it must not replace the free activity of individuals and groups but rather discipline and support them as needed
- Allow itself to be guided by the moral order, which "has God as its origin and end" (Pope John XXIII, *Pacem in Terris*, no. 47). It is precisely from this order that it derives its power to compel and its moral legitimacy, not from individual will or the desire for power.
- Recognize, respect, and promote the essential human and moral values
- Educate people to tolerance and mutual acceptance, in dialogue and cooperation for the common good

- Issue laws that are just, meaning in keeping with the dignity of the human person and the dictates of right reason. The citizen is therefore not obliged in conscience to follow the prescriptions of the civil authorities if these are contrary to the requirements of the moral order, to the fundamental rights of persons, or to the teachings of the Gospel.
- Administer punishments that are commensurate with the seriousness of the crime and intended to repair the disorder created by the offense and contribute to the correction and to the personal and social rehabilitation of the offender.

What are the criteria for healthy positive state secularism?

✠ Christ himself gave the most basic criterion for a proper conception of relations between the political sphere and the religious sphere: "Repay to Caesar what belongs to Caesar and to God what belongs to God" (Mk 12:17).

"It is fundamental, on the one hand, to insist on the distinction between the political realm and that of religion in order to preserve both the religious freedom of citizens and the responsibility of the State towards them; and, on the other hand, to become more aware of the irreplaceable role of religion for the formation of consciences and the contribution which it can bring to—among other things—the creation of a basic ethical consensus in society" (Pope Benedict XVI, Address at Elysée Palace, Paris, September 12, 2008).

✠ The secularism of the state means that

- On the one hand, the state does not espouse any particular religion, both because it has no competence in the field of religion and because it does not pursue religious aims
- On the other hand:
  - It recognizes and respects religion.
  - It promotes and fosters the broadest religious freedom possible.
  - It facilitates religious practice on the part of those who desire this, with respect for public order, public morality, and the law.
  - It considers religion not a mere individual sentiment to be confined to the private sphere alone but rather a communal public presence that enriches social life.

In doing this, the secular state recognizes and fosters the rights of citizens to practice their religion.

✠ "This is certainly not an expression of secularity, but its degeneration into secularism, hostility to every important political and cultural form of religion; and especially to the presence of any religious symbol in public institutions.

"Likewise, to refuse the Christian community and its legitimate representatives the right to speak on the moral problems that challenge all human consciences today, and especially those of legislators and jurists, is not a sign of a healthy secularity.

"Thus, it is not a question of undue meddling by the Church in legislative activity that is proper and exclusive to the State but, rather, of the affirmation and defense of the important values that give meaning to the person's life and safeguard his or her dignity. These values are human before being Christian, such that they cannot leave the Church silent and indifferent. It is her duty to firmly proclaim the truth about man and his destiny" (Pope Benedict XVI, Address to the Union of Italian Catholic Jurists, December 9, 2006).

In what way is the Church involved in politics?

✠ The Church as such is not involved in, does not identify or confuse itself with, and is not tied to any political system or party. It respects and promotes the healthy and proper secularism of the state.

The Church is not a political agent, it is not a party, it does not conduct politics. It is not its place to tell Catholics for whom or against whom they should vote but to help them to form their consciences in conformity with the truth of God.

✠ The Church does not propose concrete decisions to be made, programs to be enacted, political campaigns to be conducted, or persons for whom to vote. All of these realities are "matters of technique for which she is neither suitably equipped nor endowed by office" (Pope Pius XI, *Quadragesimo Anno*, no. 41). "The Church respects *the legitimate autonomy of the democratic order* and is not entitled to express preferences for this or that institutional or constitutional solution" (*Centesimus Annus*, no. 47).

✠ The Church and the political community, although both express themselves in visible organizational structures, are different in nature both because of their configuration and because of the ends that they pursue. The Church does not pursue economic, social, or political ends.

✠ It is true that the ends of the Church and of the state are of a different order, and that both are perfect societies, and therefore equipped with their own means and independent in their respective spheres of activity. But it is also true that both act on behalf of a common subject: the human person. Their separation therefore does not exclude their collaboration. "In their proper spheres, the political community and the Church are mutually independent and self-governing. Yet, by a different title, each serves the personal and social vocation of the same human beings" (*Gaudium et Spes*, no. 76). Distinction of roles, mutual respect, collaboration in the service of the all-embracing good of the person: these are some of the core principles of the relationship between Church and state.

✠ "Both the independence and the sovereignty of the state and the Church, as well as their reciprocal collaboration for the advancement of humanity and the good of the entire national community, are therefore reaffirmed in [the Lateran Pact]. In pursuing this aim, the Church is neither proposing goals of power for herself nor claiming privileges or aspiring to advantageous social or financial positions. Her sole purpose is to serve men and women, drawing inspiration as the supreme norm for her conduct from the words and example of Jesus Christ, who 'went about doing good and healing all' (Acts 10: 38). Consequently, the Catholic Church asks consideration for her specific nature; she also asks to be able to carry out freely her special mission" (Pope Benedict XVI, Address to the Italian ambassador, October 4, 2007).

✠ The Church is "well aware that 'fundamental to Christianity is the distinction between what belongs to Caesar and what belongs to God (cf. Mt 22:21), in other words, the distinction between Church and state' (*Deus Caritas Est*, no. 28). Not only does the Church recognize and respect this distinction and this autonomy but she rejoices in it as being a great progress of humanity and a fundamental condition for her own freedom and the fulfillment of her universal mission of salvation among all peoples. At the same time the Church feels it is her task, following the dictates of her own social doctrine, to declare 'on the basis of what is in accord with the nature of every human being' (ibid.), to reawaken moral and spiritual forces in society, helping to open 'mind and will' to the authentic demands of the common good. Thus, recalling the value not only for private but also and especially for public life of certain fundamental ethical principles, the Church contributes de facto to guaranteeing and promoting the dignity of the person and the common good of society. It is in this sense that true and proper cooperation desired between state and Church is brought about" (Pope Benedict XVI, Address to representatives of the diplomatic corps, December 13, 2008).

✠ The Church, precisely because it is at the service of every person and of the all-embracing growth of the person, can and must

- Evangelize the political order ("political" understood here in its highest sense), respecting its ends and autonomy
- Have the legal recognition of its identity and realize stable forms of relations and instruments (e.g., concordats) suitable for guaranteeing harmonious relations
- Judge political actions to the extent to which they have an ethical dimension. The Church therefore claims its freedom to express its moral judgment on every human reality when this is required for the defense of the fundamental rights of the person or for the salvation of souls.
- Help lay people, through its pastors, to
  - Form an upright Christian conscience
  - Recognize the importance and the value of politics, understood "as the highest form of social charity" (Pope Paul VI)
  - Bring Christian inspiration to temporal realities (this is a task that naturally arises for the laity from their being baptized and confirmed)
  - Participate in the building up of public life with all of its richness, its human and Christian dimensions, avoiding among other things an aversion to politics

- Instruct and illuminate, as is its proper task, the consciences of the faithful, above all of those who dedicate themselves to engagement in political life, in order that their activity may always be at the service of the person and the common good
- Serve, by expressing revealed truth, "all members of society by purifying reason, ensuring that it remains open to the consideration of ultimate truths" (Pope Benedict XVI, Address to Catholic educators, April 17, 2008)

✠ "In politics it is often necessary to opt for the practical path instead of the best one; yet, courage is required in order not to set out on every path merely because it is theoretically possible" (Cardinal Tarcisio Bertone, Address at the Jagiellonian University, September 15, 2007).

✠ "The immediate duty to act in the political sphere to build a just order in . . . society is not the Church's task as such, but rather, that of the lay faithful" (Pope Benedict XVI, Message on the occasion of the Italian Catholic Social Week, October 18, 2007), according to the competencies of each and under their autonomous responsibility.

✠ "There is a need for authentically Christian politicians but, even more so, for lay faithful who witness to Christ and the Gospel in the civil and political community" (Pope Benedict XVI, Address to the Pontifical Council for the Laity, May 21, 2010).

What are the duties of all Christians with regard to politics?

✠ They have the right and duty to be involved in politics, according to their opportunities and abilities, in order to promote a society at the service of the person, the beginning, middle, and end of all of their actions in the light of the Gospel. This right to take active part in public life for the sake of the common good arises both from the human person, who is social by nature, and from the faith, which is not to be concealed, but shared, and from society, which requires the contributions of all.

✠ They should not despise political activity or consider it irrelevant but instead see it as fundamental for the pursuit of the common good, and therefore uphold the attention and determined participation of every citizen, including the exercise of the vote.

✠ They can and must "configure social life correctly, respecting its legitimate autonomy and cooperating with other citizens according to their respective competences and fulfilling their own responsibility" (*Deus Caritas Est*, no. 29).

✠ They act in their own name (and not in that of the Church as such) in their political decisions, and at the same time

- Offer a consistent Christian witness
- Respect the legitimate multiplicity of temporal options

- Seek and promote, in certain situations, the political unity of Christians, for the defense of particular values and for the common good

✠ They are able to distinguish between political engagement and party affiliation. Although ethical principles are absolute and immutable, the action of political parties, while it must be inspired by ethical principles, does not consist in itself of the immediate realization of absolute ethical principles but in the realization of the common good as concretely possible in the context of a democratic system. In doing this, it is never possible to permit moral evil. In concrete terms, however, when it is not possible to obtain more, precisely by virtue of the search for the greatest common good concretely possible, it may be appropriate to accept a lesser good or tolerate a lesser evil.

✠ They do not adhere to or support political and social forces that are opposed to or do not pay sufficient attention to the essential principles of the Church's social doctrine.

✠ They recognize that the option of multiple political parties is always legitimate, as long as these parties do not contradict the Christian faith or values.

✠ They remember that every law has a pedagogical impact for good or for ill: it generates culture, creates mentalities, is a social benchmark for behavior, constructs the image of a country . . .

✠ They avoid indifference and disengagement, a retreat to the private sphere, surrender of representation.

According to what criteria do Christians choose a political party?

✠ Catholics are free to support or campaign for any party, but this does not mean that all platforms are equally compatible with the Christian faith and the demands of Christian life.

✠ In choosing and voting for a party and its platform, Christians make a serious moral evaluation concerning

- The national and international community: They evaluate the complex of material, moral, and spiritual goods that inspire and guide it.
- The party: They examine whether the platform, goals, means, and practical decisions of the party are in keeping with the Gospel, particularly in the following sectors: life, the family, childhood and adolescence, education, and solidarity. Not everything is in fact compatible with the faith. At the same time, it must be remembered that Christianity is a religious message and as such is addressed to all people, without distinction. It is therefore capable of inspiring different platforms, concrete decisions, which can be different and yet equally consistent with the same source of inspiration.
- Candidates: They evaluate their honesty, their political and professional competence, their ability to

dialogue with all, and their Christian witness in their personal, familial, professional, and social life.

For the Christian, what are the indispensable elements of a political platform?

✠ They are the principles founded on the primacy and centrality of the human person, for example:

- The protection of all the inalienable rights of the person, and in particular the defense of the right to life in all its phases (from conception to natural death: so "no" on abortion and euthanasia) and the protection of the rights of the human embryo (so "no" on genetic manipulation that implies the sacrifice of the human embryo, and "no" on human cloning)
- The protection of the family founded on the monogamous and indissoluble marriage between a man and a woman
- Freedom of education, and therefore the right of the parents to educate their children
- The social protection of minors
- Emancipation from the modern forms of slavery (the exploitation of prostitution, the liberalization of drug policy)
- The right to religious freedom
- Respect for social justice, subsidiarity, and solidarity
- The defense of peace (not to be confused with ideological pacifism) against any form of violence or terrorism

- The construction of a supportive world
- Respect for creation
- Intercultural and interreligious dialogue (see *Doctrinal Note on Some Questions Regarding the Participation of Catholics in Political Life*)

✠ It should be noted that these principles, although illuminated and confirmed by the faith, are inherent in human nature and thus common to all humanity and fundamental for the good of society (see Pope Benedict XVI, Address, March 30, 2006).

What are the requirements for a Christian who is elected as a member of a party?

✠ A Christian who is elected as a member of a party must meet the following requirements:

- Respect for and promotion of the essential Christian doctrines, in particular the principles of Christian social doctrine
- The exercise of the democratically conferred mandate as a service to society, as a service to the whole person and to every person, and as an exercise of charity. Charity, as a theological virtue, can and must influence politics as well with its power of illumination, with its energy of dedication, and with its capacity to serve and love the whole person and all people.
- A correct conception of social and political life, which the politician is called to serve

- Professional ethics and specific competence in the management of public affairs
- Permanent civil and political formation and education
- An exercise of the virtues that encourage political engagement as service (moral integrity, loyalty, sincerity, competence, patience, modesty, moderation . . .)
- Probity in public life, as a way to gain the trust of all and for the healthy management of affairs
- Detachment from personal interests and prestige. The Christian who enters into politics must act with disinterest, not seeking the benefit of self, group, or party, but the good of all and of each one.
- Listening to the healthy and just demands of the people before, during, and after election
- Christian honesty in his or her personal, family, and social life. There is an unbreakable connection between "good life" and "good governance."

✠ "I confirm," Benedict XVI has said, "the necessity and urgency of the evangelical formation and pastoral accompaniment of a new generation of Catholics working in politics, that they be coherent with the professed faith, that they have moral firmness, the capacity of educated judgment, professional competence and passion for service to the common good" (Address to the plenary assembly of the Pontifical Council for the Laity, November 15, 2008).

How must Catholic politicians behave with regard to an intrinsically unjust law?

If an intrinsically unjust law is proposed for the first time in the legislative assembly, it is never licit to support it, participate in a media campaign in favor of it, or vote for it. Those who actively cooperate with intrinsically unjust legislation (for example, a law in favor of abortion) also exclude themselves from the possibility of participating fully in the Eucharist, as is written in *Sacramentum Caritatis* of Benedict XVI.

If an intrinsically unjust law is already in effect, the Catholic politician must oppose it by whatever means possible and make this opposition known. If it is not possible to abrogate a law of this kind completely, he or she could licitly offer support to more restrictive proposals aimed at limiting the harm of such a law and at diminishing its negative effects on the level of culture and of public morality, on the condition that his or her absolute personal opposition to such laws be clear and known to all, and that the danger of scandal be avoided. In doing this, there is no illicit cooperation with an unjust law, but rather a legitimate and obligatory attempt to limit its harmful aspects (see *Evangelium Vitae*, no. 73).

It must never be forgotten that every law also has a didactic dimension, which means that it plays a role of educating persons, in particular the new generations, indicating the path to be followed. Civil laws are, in fact, structuring principles of human life in society, for good or for ill. They play a very important role, sometimes even decisive, in promoting a mentality and a custom. The forms of life and models expressed in them not only shape the outer contours of social life, but also tend to modify new generations' understanding and evaluation of behavior.

How must the clergy behave with regard to politics?

✠ Priests must not use their position and their mission in the Church to support a certain party, being *super partes*. He is "all things to all, in order to save all" (see 1 Cor 9:19), at the service of all and for the good of each and of all.

✠ Priests cannot be elected to any party, except when "in the judgment of competent ecclesiastical authority, the protection of the rights of the Church or the promotion of the common good requires it" (CIC, c. 287 §2).

✠ Priests must offer their constructive and consistent contribution in the "pre-political" and political (but not party-affiliated) field, proclaiming the fundamental values of the person and of the Gospel and offering guidelines and perspectives on the values that must inspire sociopolitical activity.

✠ Priests must promote good relations with political administrations in open and cordial collaboration for the good of citizens, with clearness of roles and respect for specific competencies, avoiding positions of compromise and agreements in which the autonomous position of the Church is not clear.

✠ Priests must make efforts

- Not to make spaces and structures (parishes, religious institutes, Catholic schools, and other ecclesial realities) available for the campaign purposes of individual parties or political formations

- Not to organize, shortly before elections, any initiatives of formation, reflection, prayer, or spirituality that involve persons engaged at the social and political level and party candidates
- Not to indicate what political party they believe gives the greatest guarantees in the defense and promotion of the human values in question. This indication would in reality be a recommendation to vote for a particular person.
- To ensure that parish property is not used for putting up fliers, posters, or any other form of campaign promotion, and that parish bulletins not be used for these purposes.

✠ Thus the clergy and institutions of the Church must remain completely outside of pre-election political debates and efforts, keeping absolutely outside of any party or political affiliation. For priests, this requirement is based on the very nature of their ministry (see Congregation for the Clergy, *Directory on the Ministry and Life of Priests*, no. 33, cpv. 1°: EV 14/798).

✠

For more on this topic, see the following pontifical documents:

Pope John XXIII, *Mater et Magistra*, 1961; *Pacem in Terris*, 1963

Vatican Council II, *Gaudium et Spes*, 1966, nos. 74-76

Pope John Paul II, *Sollecitudo Rei Socialis*, 1988; *Evangelium Vitae*, 1995; *Centesimus Annus*, 1991

Catechism of the Catholic Church, nos. 1897-1901; 2212-2213; 2244-2246

Compendium of the CCC, nos. 405-406, 463-465

Congregation for the Doctrine of the Faith, *Doctrinal Note on Some Questions Regarding the Participation of Catholics in Political Life*, 2002

Pontifical Council for Justice and Peace, *Compendium of the Social Doctrine of the Church*, pp. 206-232

XII
Science

What have the relations between faith and science been like down through the Church's history?

✠ Down through the centuries, there have been and still are persons who have sought out dialogue and cooperation between faith and science, on behalf of and in service to the growth of the person and of all humanity.

✠ It is also true that there has been no lack, even among Christians, of attitudes that have not sufficiently perceived and recognized the legitimate autonomy of science, prompting quarrels and controversies, to the point of maintaining that science and faith are in opposition to each other. Other times there has been indifference between them, which has led them to travel down parallel paths in complete ignorance of each other.

✠ In any case, it must also be affirmed that the Church, faithful to its mission, can enter into dialogue with any kind of science and effectively use its scientific results in order to better fulfill its mission. Sent out to all peoples, of any time and place, the Church is not bound in an exclusive and indissoluble manner to any kind of science, or to any scientific achievement.

What kind of dialogue can there be between faith and science?

✠ A dialogue in distinction: that is, a dialogue that recognizes the specific characteristics of each of the two. In fact, each one

- Has its own methods, areas, and objects of research, its own limitations and purposes (e.g., in many cases, science explains the "how," faith explains the "why")
- Must respect the other and recognize the legitimate possibility of the other to autonomous activity according to its specific principles

✠ "There are 'two orders of knowledge' which are distinct, namely, faith and reason. . . . The Church does not indeed forbid that 'when the human arts and disciplines are practiced they use their own principles and their proper method, each in its own domain.' Hence, 'acknowledging this just liberty,' this sacred Synod affirms the legitimate autonomy of human culture and especially of the sciences" (*Gaudium et Spes*, no. 36).

"Faith and reason are like two wings on which the human spirit rises to the contemplation of truth; and God has placed in the human heart a desire to know the truth" (*Fides et Ratio*, Foreword). Not only is faith not contrary to reason, it opens the eyes of reason, it expands our horizon and allows us to find the responses necessary for the challenges of different times. "A particularly urgent task of religion today is to unveil the vast potential of human reason, which is itself God's gift and which is elevated by revelation and faith. Belief in the one God, far from stunting our capacity to understand ourselves and the world, broadens it" (Pope Benedict XVI, Address to representatives of the Muslim community of Cameroon, March 19, 2009).

With regard to the relationship between science and faith, St. Thomas Aquinas stated that "all truths come from the same sun, the different rays of nature and of faith cannot contradict each other."

There are different levels of truth, and the truth of faith is not in contradiction with the truth of science. This does not mean, however, that there is not a certain dialectic, because it is not always easy to understand the truth of faith or the truth of science. In spite of the necessary circularity between faith and reason, they are not the same thing. Faith and reason do not coincide; they use different modes of understanding and their contents do not entirely coincide.

✠ At the same time, both are called to serve the person and humanity, fostering the development and the overall growth of each and of all.

How is the autonomy of science to be understood?

✠ "If by the autonomy of earthly affairs we mean that created things and societies themselves enjoy their own laws and values which must be gradually deciphered, put to use, and regulated by men, then it is entirely right to demand that autonomy. Such is not merely required by modern man, but harmonizes also with the will of the Creator. For by the very circumstance of their having been created, all things are endowed with their own stability, truth, goodness, proper laws and order. Man must respect these as he isolates them by the appropriate methods of the individual sciences or arts. . . .

✠ "But if the expression, the independence of temporal affairs, is taken to mean that created things do not depend on God, and that man can use them without any reference to their Creator, anyone who acknowledges God will see how false such a meaning is. For without the Creator the creature would disappear" (*Gaudium et Spes*, no. 36).

✠ "It is an illusion to claim moral neutrality in scientific research and its applications. On the other hand, guiding principles cannot be inferred from simple technical efficiency, or from the usefulness accruing to some at the expense of others or, even worse, from prevailing ideologies. Science and technology by their very nature require unconditional respect for fundamental moral criteria. They must be at the service of the human person, of his inalienable rights, of his true and integral good, in conformity with the plan and the will of God" (CCC, no. 2294).

✠ The autonomy of science therefore ends where the upright conscience of the scientist recognizes the evil of the method, result, or effect.

Can there be a true contrast between the discoveries of science and the truths of faith?

✠ One must overcome the opposition that has sometimes been drawn between scientific discoveries reached through reason and the truth known through the faith. There cannot be any true contradiction, as long as one is dealing with a positive scientific discovery and an authentic truth of faith. In this case, one is dealing with the same truth, which human beings reach by following complementary paths. In fact, *omnis veritas a Deo*: all truth comes from God. Both of these, science and faith, although they are distinct, are united in the truth: they converge in admitting the capacity to know truths and the Truth, they find in the truth their foundation, the reason for their existence, the aim of their activity.

✠ Both science and faith are gifts from God. "Though faith is above reason, there can never be any real discrepancy between faith and reason. Since the same God who reveals mysteries and infuses faith has bestowed the light of reason on the human mind, God cannot deny himself, nor can truth ever contradict truth" (*Dei Filius*, no. 4).

✠ "Therefore, if methodical investigation within every branch of learning is carried out in a genuinely scientific manner and in accord with moral norms, it never truly conflicts with faith. For earthly matters and the concerns of faith derive from the same God. Indeed, whoever labors to penetrate the secrets of reality with a humble and steady mind, is, even unawares, being led by the hand of God, who holds all things in existence, and gives them their identity" (*Gaudium et Spes*, no. 36). Thus in some cases, the faith can be above reason, but never contrary to it.

✠ Both are at the service of the human person, of the whole person and of all that is authentically human. They are ordered to the person, from which they draw their origin and development, and whose comprehensive development they promote for the good of all. They find in the person the indication of their end and the awareness of their respective limitations.

✠ So there is no choice between science and morality, but rather a moral use of science.

In what does the anthropological, humanistic value of science consist?

✠ It consists in the fact that science

- Is conducted by human beings
- Exists for the good of the individual person and of humanity
- Exists for the personal good of scientists themselves. In fact, all scientists, through personal study and research
    - Perfect themselves and their humanity, construct their personalities, and mold themselves
    - Travel down the path of personal encounter with the truth, in freedom and responsibility
    - Can encounter God himself, Creator of heaven and earth

✠ Science performs a valuable service for others, for society, and for the Church itself.

What positive contribution does science make to society and to the Church?

✠ There are many positive aspects that science can offer, such as

- Rigorous fidelity to the truth in scientific investigation
- Collaboration with others in specialized technical groups
- The sense of international solidarity
- An ever more lively sense of responsibility on the part of experts in helping and protecting humanity
- The intention of making living conditions better for all, especially for those who suffer for various reasons
- The great contribution that it can offer in elevating the human family to the highest conceptions of truth, goodness, and beauty, and to a vision of the things of universal value
- Assistance to faith in purifying itself from mistaken elements
- The expression and actualization of human lordship over creation. Science implements the plan of God, manifested at the beginning of time, of subduing the earth and perfecting creation.
- The fulfillment of the great commandment of Christ to spend oneself in the service of one's brothers and

sisters: "Whatever you did for one of these least brothers of mine, you did for me" (Mt 25:40).

✠ All of these positive aspects that science presents are

- A wonderful product of human creativity and of the insatiable appetite for seeking and exploration that is present in the human person
- A sign of the greatness of God
- A fruit of the ineffable divine plan, which God has entrusted to human beings, concerning creation
- A preparation to receive the proclamation of the Gospel

What can faith contribute to science?

✠ The Christian faith offers science excellent encouragement and assistance to perform its task with greater commitment, and especially to discover the full meaning of its activities, within and in service to the complete vocation of the human person

✠ The Christian faith helps science to be more aware of its limitations:

- It is not the highest value to which all others must submit.
- It cannot explain everything, and above all it cannot explain everything about the human person. Science can give a partial and non-exhaustive answer to the problem of the truth about human beings, considered

in all their dimensions, on their ultimate existential questions, and on the ultimate meaning of our history and that of the universe.

- It cannot give answers to theological or philosophical problems, since it is limited to experiential knowledge.

✠ The Christian faith also warns about the serious risks that science can incur. For example, "today's progress in science and technology can foster a certain exclusive emphasis on observable data, and an agnosticism about everything else. For the methods of investigation which these sciences use can be wrongly considered as the supreme rule for discovering the whole truth. By virtue of their methods, however, these sciences cannot penetrate to the intimate meaning of things. Yet the danger exists that man, confiding too much in modern discoveries, may even think that he is sufficient unto himself and no longer seek any higher realities" (*Gaudium et Spes*, no. 57).

✠ The Christian faith attributes the greatest importance to the authentic achievements of science. In fact, the faith affirms that although one must carefully distinguish earthly progress from the development of the Kingdom of Christ, nevertheless scientific progress, to the extent to which it can contribute to better ordering human society, contributes to realizing the Kingdom of God, to building "new heavens" and a "new earth" (2 Pt 3:13). "The dialogue between faith and reason, religion and science, does not only make it possible to show people of our time the reasonableness of faith in God as effectively and convincingly as possible, but also to demonstrate that the definitive fulfillment of every authentic human aspiration rests in Jesus Christ. In this regard, a serious evangelizing effort cannot ignore the questions that arise also from today's scientific and philosophical discoveries" (Pope Benedict XVI, Address to the plenary assembly of the CDF, February 10, 2006).

✠ The Christian faith offers the moral priorities and principles that science must respect. "Science, moreover, is unable to work out ethical principles; it can only accept them and recognize them as necessary to eradicate its potential pathologies. In this context, philosophy and theology become indispensable aids which must be placed alongside science in order to prevent it from proceeding on its own down a twisting path, full of unexpected accidents and not without risks. This does not mean restricting scientific research or preventing technology from producing the means for development; rather, it consists in maintaining vigilance about the sense of responsibility that reason possesses in regards to science, so that it stays on track in its service to the human being" (Pope Benedict XVI, Address on the 10th anniversary of *Fides et Ratio*, October 16, 2008).

What priorities must science follow?

✠ Science must allow itself to be guided by the primacy of

- The person over things
- Ethics over technology
- Spirit over matter
- Being over having and doing

- The search for the truth
- The demands of justice and peace

✠ It must therefore avoid pursuing priorities established mainly by

- Economic motives (the indiscriminate search for personal or group economic profit)
- The interests of political groups
- The search for personal prestige

What are the moral principles that science must respect?

✠ Here are some fundamental moral principles:

- Not all that is scientifically and technologically feasible is also morally acceptable.
- It is not just to obtain good through evil.
- The end does not justify the means.

✠ Respect must therefore be shown to

- The comprehensive good of the human person and of humanity
- The transcendent dimension of the person and of creation itself
- The life and dignity of human beings, their quality of life, the rights of current and future generations
- Creation and the environment

Are moral principles a hindrance for science?

Moral principles are not a hindrance or an obstacle to progress, but "the stream bed through which the impetuous current of human thought and action must run.

"Ethics puts limitations on science in order to increase its power, its utility, and its efficacy, in order to keep it from overflowing its banks, flooding and destroying. Ethics is an element that has contributed to all the best and most beautiful things that the human person has produced" (Pope Pius XII, Address to the First International Congress on the Histopathology of the Nervous System, September 14, 1952).

What is the task of science?

✠ To discover the wonders of nature, with that attitude that is proper to the one who does not stretch out his or her hand over the world saying, "It is mine," but of the one who, in amazement, sees it being extended by another and recognizes that it is a gift from an Other for all.

✠ To respect the ontological and axiological difference that exists between the human person and other living beings.

✠ To respect the nature of each being and of its mutual connection with other beings in an ordered and balanced system (the ecosystem).

✠ To promote the environment as a home and as a resource for the human person and for all human beings.

✠ To seek the good of humanity according to the plan of God and his will, and to allow the human person, considered as an individual and as a member of society, to cultivate and actualize his or her complete vocation.

✠ To perform a service to

- The truth
- The dignity of the person and to his or her quality of life
- Humanity and its values
- The satisfaction of basic human needs above all, seeking always to wipe out hunger and disease in particular

✠ To preserve the human faculties of contemplation and admiration that lead to wisdom.

✠ To achieve a form of scientific progress that may be true human progress.

✠ To avoid

- Believing that it can solve everything
- Absolutizing its own method and results
- Excluding other paths of research
- Using the earth in an arbitrary manner, subjecting it without reservation to its will, exploiting the resources of creation recklessly
- Experimenting on human beings without the explicit consent of the subjects or their legal guardians, or

creating disproportionate or avoidable risks for the lives or physical integrity of the subjects

✠ To look with interest at the Christian faith, which reveals the ultimate meaning of human dignity and leads to an encounter with Christ, the perfect man, in following whom the human person also becomes more fully human and finds fullness and completion in him.

What is the task of the scientist?

As a human being, he or she has the task of

- Taking into account the role of science, its purposes, its limitations
- Respecting the moral principles presented above, fulfilling ethical responsibilities, remembering that he or she is a human being first and a scientist after
- Avoiding the risk of dehumanizing other human beings
- Remembering that he or she is not the absolute master of himself or herself, of his or her life
- Respecting the psychological and physical integrity of self and others
- Pondering
  - The general meaning of one's quest for knowledge
  - The method followed (the end does not justify the means)
  - The final result and the consequences that the results achieved could have on the level of application

    - The moral validity of one's activity
    - Creation as a reflection of God, a place where the greatness, the goodness, the providence of God are revealed
- Avoiding "specialist compartmentalization," instead seeking synthesis:
    - Connecting the plurality of achievements
    - Integrating them into the general sense of life
    - Harmonizing them with the ethical-moral vision

"The segmentation of knowledge, with its splintered approach to truth and consequent fragmentation of meaning, keeps people today from coming to an interior unity" (*Fides et Ratio*, no. 85).

What is the task of the public authorities with regard to science?

The public authorities, as guardians of the common good, must

- Ensure that research is directed to the good of persons and of society and to the protection of the environment
- Moderate and reconcile the pressures of divergent interests
- Make just laws that protect the good of the person and of society with respect for moral principles
- Monitor the effects of technological or scientific discoveries

- Publish guidelines, including for the respect of the integrity and rhythms of nature, because natural resources are limited and some of them are not renewable
- Actively support fields of research that are not financed by private interests, setting aside public funds in keeping with the principles of subsidiarity
- Prevent research that harms human life and dignity or that ignores the needs of the poorest peoples of the world, who in general are less equipped for scientific research

What is the role of the Church with regard to science?

✠ To proclaim the contribution that faith makes to science.

✠ To train qualified commentators in the fields of the physical or life sciences, theology, and the philosophy of science, capable of communicating over the Internet, radio, or television on points of friction that may arise between science and faith.

✠ To create networks of communication among Catholic students appreciated for their professional capacities and their fidelity to the Magisterium, as well as among scientific academies, associations of experts in technology, and episcopal conferences.

✠ To foster widely distributed Catholic publications that benefit from the contributions of persons truly qualified in these fields

✠ To implement a pastoral strategy aimed at encouraging and fostering a profound spiritual life in scientists.

✠

For more on this topic, see the following pontifical documents:

Vatican Council I, *Dei Filius*
Vatican Council II, *Gaudium et Spes*
Pope John Paul II, *Fides et Ratio*, 1998
Catechism of the Catholic Church, nos. 159; 2293-2294
Compendium of the CCC, nos. 475-477
Pontifical Council for Justice and Peace, *Compendium of the Social Doctrine of the Church*, nos. 331-363; 456-473